W9-CUO-780

CISTERCIAN STUDIES SERIES: NUMBER TWO HUNDRED TWENTY–SEVEN

Emma Cazabonne

A Light to Enlighten the Darkness

CISTERCIAN STUDIES SERIES: NUMBER TWO HUNDRED TWENTY-SEVEN

A Light to Enlighten the Darkness

Daily Readings for Meditation during the Winter Season

by

Emma Cazabonne

Cistercian Publications
Kalamazoo, Michigan

Texts have been adapted from various works
in the Cistercian Fathers Series
Cistercian Publications 1970-2008

© Anthology copyrighted 2008 by Cistercian Publications

The work of Cistercian Publications has been made possible
in part by support from Western Michigan University
to the Institute of Cistercian Studies

Library of Congress Cataloging-in-Publication Data

A light to enlighten the darkness : daily readings for meditation during
the winter season / [edited] by Emma Cazabonne.
    p. cm. — (Cistercian studies series ; no. 227)
  · Includes bibliographical references (p.   ) and index.
    ISBN 978-0-87907-227-8 (pbk.)
  1. Catholic Church—Prayers and devotions.   2. Light—Religious
aspects—Catholic Church—Meditations.   I. Cazabonne, Emma.
II. Title.   III. Series.

  BX2182.3.L54 2008
  242'.2—dc22   2008011414

Printed in the United States of America.

To John and to my Greek Orthodox family;
to Mothers Aelred, Marie-Rose, Gail, Nettie,
and to all my cistercian brothers and sisters;
to Anne, who led me to the Taboric light.

The Contents

Foreword

God is light, says Saint John, and in him there is no darkness at all (1 Jn 1:5). This is a terrifying concept, for it means that in the presence of God there is no concealment, no hiding place, and all our manifold imperfections are revealed in that shadowless and, in one sense, merciless light. 'What is more terrible to sinners', asks Geoffrey of Auxerre, 'than to appear before the face of the Sun of Justice shining with full strength?' (Mar 16[1]). And that we are all sinners is manifestly obvious, though not always to ourselves.

Four centuries or so after Saint John, pseudo-Dionysius takes up the same theme, but gives it a different nuance. He lists light as one of the divine names of God, and sees in the finite and visible sun a symbol of the infinite and invisible deity. Just as the sun illumines all things, so too does God. He gives his light to all who can receive it in the measure in which they can receive it—John of Forde would agree (Dec 30)—and it is his light that creates us, gives us life, preserves us, and perfects us. By illuminating our minds, he drives out ignorance, and the more we yearn for his light, the more he bestows it.[2] For pseudo-Dionysius, therefore, God's light is a creative and illuminating power which is a manifestation, a true revelation, of God himself.

Five hundred years after pseudo-Dionysius another eastern writer takes up the same subject, and leaves in no doubt whatever that God and light are inseparable. Which writer? Symeon the New Theologian (949–1022), a monk of the great monastery of the Studios in Constantinople. Abbot of Saint Mamas in the same city, he ended his days as a contentious hermit in a small ruined oratory on the other side of the Bosphorus. God's light, Symeon tells us,

> shines around us without any diminution, without change, without alteration, without form. It speaks, works, lives and gives life, and transforms into light those whom it enlightens. It is we who bear witness that God is light (1 Jn 1:5), and those deemed worthy to see him have all seen him as light. Those who have received him have received him as light, for the light of his glory goes before him and it is impossible for him to appear without light. Those who have not seen his light have not seen him, for he is the light, and those who have not received the light have not yet received grace.[3]

Symeon's unequivocal views anticipate what would later develop into a violent controversy which first divided the eastern Church and then had a profound impact on its theology. The controversy was the Hesychast Controversy, and the essential question at issue was not whether God is light—that was clear from no less an authority than Saint John himself—but exactly what sort of light he is. More precisely, if a Christian mystic experienced God as light, did he or she experience the uncreated light of God or created light? The difference is of first importance. If we may use an analogy, it is rather like the difference between holding the hand of a living person, and holding a plaster cast of that person's hand. In the former case, we are actually in contact with the person—indeed, in a certain sense, we are in contact with the whole person, since the hand is an integral part of the body—but in the latter case, the contact is merely symbolic. It is the same with God's light. If we experience the uncreated light, then we are in contact with God; and if we are in contact with God, we may participate in his divine attributes: his goodness, beauty, knowledge, joy, perfection. The more we participate, the more like God we become; and although we can never become God—the creature can never become the Creator—we can become, as William of Saint Thierry puts it, 'what God is' (*quod Deus est*).[4] Such is the nature of what the eastern theologians—and a few westerners (including William and Bernard of Clairvaux)—refer to as 'deification'. But if we experience only the created light, that vital contact is missing, participation is impossible, and deification cannot be achieved.

Note, too, Symeon's emphasis on transformation. God's light 'transforms into light those whom it enlightens', and

Symeon himself experienced this, not once, but many times. He was, we might say, a 'natural mystic', and could never quite understand why others were not. On one occasion, when he was praying and saying silently 'God, have mercy on me, a sinner' (Lk 18:13), a divine light suddenly filled the room. He lost all consciousness of where he was and saw nothing but light. Indeed, it seemed to him that he had been united with the light, transformed into light, and that he had left this world altogether. He was overcome with tears and filled with an inexpressible joy.[5] The same principle, though with less detail, appears in Gertrud the Great (see Dec 22), John of Forde (Jan 28), and Gilbert of Hoyland. 'Anyone on whom your lightning flashes', says Gilbert, 'becomes a flash of lightning. Anyone on whom you shed a ray of your light, you make like yourself' (Feb 7). For those who followed Symeon, the light they experienced was understood to be the light of the Transfiguration on Mount Tabor, but it is rare to find this idea in the west. Isaac of Stella, always individual (and always difficult), approaches it when he speaks of the mind soaring above all corporeality into the realm of the incorporeal and the unseen (Jan 21–22). There, as if on Mount Tabor, 'it gazes on Jesus, Jesus transfigured, glorified', but the experience is too much for us. We cannot tolerate that glory, and our reason, intellect, and understanding fall on their faces (Jan 23).

On the whole, however, we do not find in the west the same profound theology of light as we do in the east, but what we do find—as is clear from this rich anthology—is deeply rewarding. Indeed, the only reason we can respond to the light at all is because of what Augustine called the *scintilla rationis*, the 'little spark of reason',[6] which is the key to our creation in the image of God. From being children of darkness, we are called to be children of light (Mar 10); and if God himself dwells in light unapproachable (1 Tim 6:16: the phrase occurs again and again), he sent his Son to us to be the light of the Church in a dark world (Jan 6/3, Jan 13). 'From Him to his whole Church', says John of Forde, 'emanates all the radiance there is' (Feb 21), although—alas!—the Church has not always opened its eyes to that light. Yet if his light is his grace—and Isaac of Stella tells us that it is (Jan 25)—then, in and through that grace, we may be enlightened. The light of grace is the dawn of the spiritual day, and it leads us from the darkness of ignorance and ill-will into the daylight of wisdom, virtue, and justice: the daylight of Christ himself (Jan 25). But let us remember at all costs that this enlightenment is not for us alone. Our business in this world is not to seek our own selfish illumination. The light of charity (or the light that is charity), says John of Forde, shines internally for itself, but shines outwardly for others (Feb 13), and it is a standard theme of medieval spirituality that you cannot love God unless you also love your neighbour. Few are clearer on this point than Baldwin of Forde. We should not flatter ourselves, he tells us, that we love God, we should not deceive ourselves in thinking that we love God, if we do not love our neighbour, for the love of God is 'made known, strengthened, and fortified' in the love of our neighbour.[7]

The Christian path is not simply a quest for personal illumination, but a demand that that illumination be put into practice. If we have the light of Christ in our heart (Feb 12), it is there to shine both for ourselves and for others. If, by the light of God's grace, we are enabled to see more clearly, it is so that we may see more clearly how we may serve our neighbour. If God is the life-giving light which instructs our minds by his wisdom and truth (Jan 4), that is not for our own selfish enjoyment. As Bernard of Clairvaux tells us, when the soul loses the light of contemplation (and that light is always rare and fleeting),

> she does not permit herself to fall into the darkness of sin or the idleness of sloth, but holds herself within the light of good works. And that you might know that good works are light, Christ said *Let your light shine before others* (Mt 5:16); and there is no doubt that this was said about works that others could see with their eyes. (Feb 29)

As Watkin Williams observed long ago, 'the mystic life is no less morally obligated by the life of justification, at every stage of its growth, than is the latter the instinctive expression of the former'.[8]

And who are our neighbours to whom we owe such devotion? Everyone, both good and bad alike, for God's light shines on all (Feb 24). And not only does it shine on all—good and bad, just and unjust—it shines on all equally and freely (Feb 25), and that is something which it is too easy (and too convenient) to forget. It is true that we live in darkness, and many passages in this anthology testify to that. We read of the darkness of ignorance, of sin, of our separation from God, of mistaken opinions, of errors, of ungodliness, of unbelief, of this world in general. But the light shines in the darkness, and the darkness has not overcome it (Jn 1:5). Our business is to do all that we can to help shed that light, and the task is difficult, demanding, sometimes unpleasant, and often wholly unrewarding.

We are not, however, alone in our efforts. The Christian church of the Middle Ages, both eastern and western, had no doubt whatever that help was needed and that help was available. The greatest help, of course, comes from the ever-Virgin Mother of God, the *Theotokos* or 'God-bearer' of eastern Christianity, the unique castle which Jesus entered (Dec 29), the Star of the Sea. And whoever calls on her (says Saint Bernard) will never despair:

> Keeping her in your thoughts, you will never wander away. With your hand in hers, you will never stumble. With her protecting you, you will not be afraid. With her leading you, you will never tire. (Jan 1)

After Mary come the saints, and apart from illuminating our paths with their own light (Feb 24), the saints also offer us models, exemplars, to imitate (Feb 23). 'Follow the guiding light of the Fathers who have gone before you', says Guerric of Igny: it is the straightest way to find Jesus (Feb 3). But to imitate the saints is no small demand and no small task. 'I want you to be like Saint John', says Bernard of

Clairvaux (Feb 22), and the fact that we are most unlikely to succeed in this endeavour is irrelevant. God does not expect us to succeed; he expects us to try. Once again, it is Baldwin of Forde who sets forth the matter with eminent clarity:

> If it be granted me from above to love God and love my neighbour, then even though my own merits are poor and meagre, I have a hope which is above and beyond all my merits. I am certain that through the communion of love the merits of the saints will profit me and that the communion of the saints can make good my own imperfection and insufficiency.[9]

Sometimes, it seems, God's light can overwhelm a soul and ravish it into an experience and state of being which cannot be described. We are told that the body of Ida of Louvain was 'bathed all over with a light so bright as to gleam like some unearthly substance' (Mar 3)—so bright, in fact, that the poor sister who witnessed the event thought she had been struck blind (Mar 3). 'Fiery rays, like sunbeams' shone forth from Ida's face, and 'after Communion, the gaze of her eyes would become so lightsome and bright that the objects on which she focused them would themselves begin to emit a brilliant glow, which you observe for yourself' (Mar 4). Gertrud the Great of Helfta felt the light which came from Christ's 'deifying eyes' penetrate her very being and produce in all her limbs 'an extraordinarily supernatural effect' (Feb 6). John of Forde seems to have experienced something similar, but he is far more discreet (Jan 14).

Sometimes the experience was simply ineffable, utterly overwhelming (Feb 2), and one entered what pseudo-Dionysius described as a 'dazzling darkness' which was beyond light as we know it. There our blinded intellect is filled and over-filled 'with the utterly intangible and invisible nature of splendours beyond all beauty'.[10] This, for any Christian, is clearly the summit of the spiritual path, and from the time of the early Church it has been regarded as a true foretaste of the Beatific Vision. On the other hand, as we have said, it is an experience as fleeting as it is infrequent—even Bernard, who was no stranger to ecstatic raptures, twice describes it as 'extremely rare' (*rarissimus*)[11]—and it also possesses a less pleasant aspect. As Baldwin tells us,

> if it should happen that we experience just a taste (*modicum*) of something good, it only serves to remind us of our misery, for what we experience is rare and superficial, and in no way complete.[12]

Our misery is the result of our unlikeness to our Maker. Created as we are in the image of God, we have besmirched that image with the dross of sin, and dwell now in the 'land of unlikeness', the *regio dissimilitudinis*.[13] And if a single ray of the divine light should shine upon us, it will reveal all too clearly our manifold deformities and inadequacy (Mar 1). And how do we deal with this? The Christian Church, both east and west, has been (for once) united in its answer: strive to regain the lost likeness, strive to become more like God. Few are clearer on this point than Bernard of Clairvaux. The more we are enlightened, the more like God we become; the more like God we become, the more clearly do we see him; and when we are wholly like him, then we shall see him as he is, face to face (Feb 9, Feb 27, Mar 8). 'Do not be like the world', says Bernard, 'be like the Word!' (Feb 20). In the eastern church, as we have seen, the process is known as deification, 'becoming like God', and it is a process which begins here and now, this very minute, though it continues forever.

It is improbable that many of us will experience the true foretaste of the Beatific Vision here on earth, that 'divine inebriation' which overcame Ida and Gertrud (Mar 2, Mar 9).[14] It is equally improbable that many of us will see 'the whole world gathered up in a single ray of light' (Dec 21). Few of us are 'natural mystics' like Symeon the New Theologian, and it would be unwise to go to Communion in the expectation of experiencing what Ida experienced (Mar 9). But so what? The spiritual path in general, and the monastic spiritual path in particular, is not an unending quest for 'spiritual highs' and paramystical phenomena. It is, rather, an unending quest for God, and loss of self is better understood not in an ontological way, when (if we may quote the great Teresa), the soul flows into God as a tiny stream enters the sea,[15] but as the loss of self-will, that self-centredness and egocentricity which so often and so effectively prevents us from being illumined by the light of the knowledge of God. God's rebuke to Bernard is absolutely to the point: 'Why should you want to see Me in My splendour, while you still do not know yourself?' (Mar 8). But 'if we cannot behold the wonders reserved for the life to come', says Bernard, 'we may at least contemplate something of the marvels accomplished for us on earth' (Jan 5). One may ask, in fact, if the momentary, rare, ecstatic experience of God himself is the aim and goal of the Christian path, why Christ ever bothered to become incarnate at all. In Jesus of Nazareth we see 'the splendour of glory and brightness of eternal Light in the clay vessel of our flesh' (Jan 6/2), and Saint Gregory Palamas, the 'Light of Orthodoxy', made it eminently clear that when the Second Person of the Trinity became flesh, he also became matter. In and through the Incarnation, the whole of material creation was redeemed and sanctified, and our purpose in this life is not the selfish pursuit of Altered States of Consciousness, but the manifestation of the principle of the Incarnation in our own lives.

Our business in this world, in fact, is to cultivate the light of the virtues—faith, hope, temperance, and prudence—and with their help (says Aelred),

> let the light of wisdom shine like the splendour of the sun, and let the light of spiritual knowledge, which waxes in some of us and wanes in others, appear like the beauty of the moon. (Jan 19)

Our task is the pursuit of wisdom, truth, holiness, and goodness (Feb 1); and if, in the course of this pursuit, God decides to bestow upon us the hyper-light of ecstasy, so be it. If he does not, so be it. If he is indeed God, he presumably knows what he is doing. We, all too often, do not. However enlightened we may be, we are still in darkness; and if we are enlightened at all, the little light we have only makes us realize that we need to be enlightened yet more. The greater the light shed by our own lamp, says Guerric of Igny,

> the more truly does the lamp itself reveal our darkness. . . . The measure of our enlightenment remains this: that those who are able to know their own inadequacy and recognize what is lacking in them are judged as having made great progress towards the light of truth. (Mar 1)

'I do not ask to see / The distant scene', wrote Cardinal Newman, 'one step enough for me.'[16] Step by step, seeing light in His light (Dec 22, Jan 6/2, Mar 12), we may make our slow progress towards the end for which we were created. Let us, therefore, fix our sight on the Sun of Righteousness (Jan 20), ask that our hearts and minds be illumined and cleansed by him, pray that the light of the Mother of God and the saints may help us in our quest, seek to show forth what little light we have in our love for our neighbours, clothe ourselves in the light of the virtues, and pray, again with Newman, a simple prayer: 'Lead, kindly light, amid the encircling gloom, / Lead thou me on.'[17]

David N. Bell

Feast of Saint Macarius the Great 2008

Notes to the Foreword

1. The references are to the passages in the anthology.

2. Ps.-Dionysius, *De div. nom.*, iv.5-6. [*On the Divine Names;* an English translation by Colm Luibheid is available in *Pseudo-Dionysius: The Complete Works* (New York-Mahwah, 1987) 47–131].

3. Symeon the New Theologian, ed. Basile Krivochéine, *Catéchèses* 28, 106–115; SCh 113:136.

4. William of Saint-Thierry, ed. Jean Déchanet, *Lettre aux Frères du Mont-Dieu* §258; SCh 223: 348 [*The Golden Epistle* CF 12:94].

5. Symeon's autobiographical account, written in the third person, appears in his *Catéchèses* 22.88-100; SCh 104: 372.

6. Augustine of Hippo, *De civ. Dei*, XXII.24.2. [*The City of God*]

7. Baldwin of Forde, Sermon 15.62; CCCM 99:244 [*Baldwin of Forde: Spiritual Tractates* XV, CF 41:179].

8. Watkin Williams, *The Mysticism of S. Bernard of Clairvaux* (London, 1931) p. 35.

9. Baldwin of Forde, Sermon 15.88; CCCM 99:251 [CF 41:190].

10. Ps.-Dionysius, *De myst. theol.*, i. [*The Mystical Theology;* Luibheid, 133–141].

11. Bernard of Clairvaux, *De grat. et lib. arb.*, v.15; SBOp 3:177 [*On Grace and Free Choice*, CF 19A:71]; *In Cant., serm.* 69.2; SBOp 2:202 [*Sermon 69.2 On the Song of Songs*, CF 40:28].

12. Baldwin of Forde, Sermon 17.9; CCCM 99:271; CF 41:50.

13. See Étienne Gilson, trans. A. H. C. Downes, *The Mystical Theology of Saint Bernard* (London–New York, 1940; rpt. Kalamazoo, 1990), Chapter Two (pp. 33–59).

14. There are interesting and instructive parallels to be drawn between such ideas as these and the 'drunken' (*sukr* in Arabic) stream of Muslim mysticism.

15. Teresa of Avila, *The Interior Castle*, VII.2.4.

16. John Henry Newman, 'Lead kindly light', verse 1.

17. *Ibid.*

The Cistercians and the Theology of Light

AN INTRODUCTION

CLAIRVAUX, Chiaravalle, Vauclair, Clairlieu, Clairmont, La Clarté-Dieu, l'Étoile. . . . These are just a few among many cistercian monasteries having a name connected with clarity, with brightness, with light.

This did not happen by chance. It is the logical reflection of what is manifested in medieval cistercian architecture. Following a bernardine inspiration, the greatest abbey churches included an elevation of the nave—normally a two-story elevation—to allow more apertures and direct light. Around 1147 and again in 1182,[1] the General Chapter itself, the legislative body of the Cistercian Order, required *albus*—white or clear—glass for the church windows, what we now call *grisaille* (grey) glass; this again was to ensure a maximum of light.

1

Still today when we enter for instance the abbey church of Pontigny in France, we feel overwhelmed by the flood of light. We find the same architectural principle in the conception of the chapter room—where the community met daily—and the refectory: both were designed in a way to allow direct light to illuminate the rooms.

The soul of cistercian architecture is obviously not color, but light. The mystical play of light on stone reflects the glorious and eternal beauty of Christ in our passing world. Christ is the Word, and the light of the world,[2] and 'the spirituality expressed in cistercian architecture is one of place, word, and light.'[3]

Indeed this luminous effect is itself the manifestation of something profound, for there is a meaningful relationship between cistercian spirituality and the environment the monks create. Their way of life, their way of relating to God, influences greatly their architecture. The latter is the external manifestation of the former.

This needs to be set in the medieval context. Among the most influential ideas of the twelfth century M.-D. Chenu identified 'the image of light everywhere zealously employed, as well by mathematicians as by men of literary bent'.[4] The note he appended to this assertion reveals that the idea permeated the domains of metaphysics, patristics, theology, and liturgy.

More recently, Emero Stiegman has demonstrated that light imagery was indeed very important in the twelfth century.[5] Bernard of Clairvaux summed up this conviction most expressively, estimating, along with the evangelist Saint John, that the experience of God can be spoken of only in terms of light and darkness.[6] In fact, Guerric of Igny, Aelred of Rievaulx, Gilbert of Hoyland, and William of Saint-Thierry[7] exulted as much as Bernard did[8] in the imagery of light. Many other generations of cistercian monks and nuns did too, if we judge by the elements of light present in their liturgical hymns.

John Morson and Hilary Costello[9] have also emphasized a traditional theology of enlightenment present in the teaching of Guerric of Igny. Guerric seemed to have delighted in a theology of light, characteristic of cistercian teaching, by going so far as to develop a fourfold enlightenment in his sermons on Epiphany. He discerns four stages of spiritual progress, each of which is called light: light of faith, light of justice, light of knowledge, and light of wisdom.[10]

A modern example will suffice to show that this is still a preponderant dimension of cistercian spirituality. Thomas Merton, deeply rooted in the teaching of our Fathers, wrote in 1964 that:

> The true call to monastic contemplation is . . . a call to renounce all that opposes this 'ineffable light' of God in Christ, to submit totally and without reservation to the light of Christ, to accept one's own helplessness and one's own deficiency, indeed one's own impurity and darkness in the presence of his light, and yet to seek with all one's heart to become transformed

3

by contemplation and love into the very purity of the light itself.[11]

Here again, the monastic quest is evoked in terms of light and darkness: a struggle in which, little by little, light will conquer all darkness in us, until we are all transformed into the image and likeness of our Creator, 'the Father of lights'.[12]

To use the concise expression of Dom Augustine Roberts, one can affirm: 'The mysticism of light in the first Cistercians . . . has remained the characteristic of cistercian spirituality'.[13]

To cite but one well-known example of contemporary cistercian architecture, I point to the restructuring of the new abbey church of Cîteaux, inaugurated in March 1998. The young architect, Denis Ouaillarbourou, has spent a great deal of time living with the brothers and reading the Cistercian Fathers. In an article describing the entire project, he lists 'light' as the first of five requirements.[14] One of the most striking results of his work is probably what he calls *les puits de lumière,* mines of light. In other words, by means of a new architectural device, he aimed at the same thing as the medieval cistercian architects did: to allow as much natural light as possible to invade the place of prayer. And I can testify that he has succeeded in doing so. His own explanation gives an idea of the preponderance of light in an example of modern cistercian architecture.[15] Light does not seem foreign either to the minimalist architect John Pawson in his design of the new cistercian foundation in Czech Republic, Nový Dvůr.

4

Sharing the same attraction with our Cistercian Fathers and Mothers without knowing it, I felt irresistibly drawn to divine light as early as my first observership in a cistercian monastery. I began then to copy anything I could find on light, and after almost twenty years of monastic life my notes have come to fill three compact and dense notebooks. I exploited some of the captivating mines of light in two little articles on light in Bernard.[16] And following up on my article on Gregory Palamas,[17] the father who synthesized so brilliantly the teaching of the eastern christian tradition on taboric light, I plan, in a future study, to show light as a common element between byzantine and cistercian spirituality.

This volume is a humble beginning, a simple sharing of my notebooks. It focuses uniquely on cistercian spirituality. The following texts, all excerpted from cistercian works, aim at nourishing the love of light, the light of the world to come, the light who is our God, the God who shines in our hearts, the divine light which has attracted our Cistercian Mothers and Fathers as many other spiritual men and women.

I have included a variety of cistercian authors: eleven monks and three nuns. I could have chosen many other texts. The collection actually begins with an exception: a text by Gregory the Great on Saint Benedict, the legislator of the Cistercians. Then there are sermons commenting on the Song of Songs by Bernard of Clairvaux, Gilbert of Hoyland, and John of Forde, the three successive cistercian commentators of that biblical book, as well as excerpts of liturgical sermons written by Cistercian Fathers from the first and second generations, and passages written by cistercian nuns. Each text is preceded by a title which I have added.

To avoid a heavy presentation, I have avoided using a system of footnotes to identify biblical quotations and have instead used simple notations. I have included only biblical citations related to light.

Originally conceived to follow the genre of the traditional *century,* a collection of a hundred texts, this *florilegium*[18] has instead taken the form of an original schema more suited to modern minds.

In the northern hemisphere, winter is characterized by few hours of natural sunlight. The winter darkness very much affects human beings. Scientists and physicians acknowledge that our body and mind can be upset by what is now termed 'seasonal affective disorder'. Likewise, I believe, our spiritual health can be affected by exposure to inner darkness. Cistercian spirituality, grounded in a positive anthropology, is light oriented. I have therefore chosen to offer one cistercian text on light for each day of the winter season, to help our minds focus on the light of Christ, and remain steadfast in hope during the gloomy winter season.

This choice makes the book relevant for all Christians, independently of their respective liturgical calendars. I have taken the liberty of proposing three texts for the two days most related to light in the christian tradition: December 25th, Christmas, and January 6th, Epiphany or Theophany.

When the Russian pilgrim met the monk who introduced him to the Jesus Prayer, he was given a nice image: the monk said to him that the *Philokalia* was like a piece of glass which enabled us to contemplate the sun present in Scriptures, just as we use a little glass to protect our eyes to look at the sun.[19] May this collection also be a humble and useful tool to attract you, the reader, to the light present in our Cistercian Fathers and Mothers, to help you love the eternal Sun who shines through their writings, and to enable you to 'walk as children of the light'.[20]

Introduction Notes

1. Chrysogonus Waddell, *Twelfth-Century Statutes From the Cistercian General Chapter.* Studia et Documenta 12 (Brecht: Cîteaux, Commentarii Cistercienses, 2002) 71 and 101.

2. See Jn 8:12 and 9:5.

3. Terryl N. Kinder, *Cistercian Europe, Architecture of Contemplation* (Grand Rapids: Eerdmans Publishing Company—Kalamazoo: Cistercian Publications, 2002) 12.

4. M.-D. Chenu, *Nature, Man, and Society in the Twelfth Century: Essays on New Theological Perspectives in the Latin West* (Chicago: University of Chicago Press, 1968) 51–52.

5. Emero Stiegman, 'The Light Imagery of Saint Bernard's Spirituality'. *The Joy of Learning and the Love of God: Essays in Honor of Jean Leclercq,* E. Rozanne Elder ed. Cistercian Studies series 160 (Kalamazoo: Cistercian Publications, 1995) 327–388.

6. As demonstrated by Stiegman, 'The Light Imagery', 352–62.

7. Stiegman, 'The Light Imagery', 335.

8. Stiegman, 'The Light Imagery', 350–351.

9. In Guerric of Igny, *Liturgical Sermons,* Volume One. Cistercian Fathers series 8. Introduction and translation by Monks of Mount Saint Bernard Abbey.

7

(Spencer:Cistercian Publications—Shannon: Irish University Press, 1971) xxxviii–xlvi.

10. *Lumen fidei, lumen iustitiae, lumen scientiae, lumen sapientiae.* Guerric d'Igny, *Sermons,* Tome 1. Sources Chrétiennes, 166. Introduction, texte critique et notes par John Morson et Hilary Costello. Traduction sous la direction de Placide Deseille. (Paris: Le Cerf, 1970). 3ème sermon 3, 276, 98–99.

11. Thomas Merton, 'The humanity of Christ in Monastic Prayer' in *Monastic Studies* 2 (Berryville, Virginia: 1964) 19–22.

12. James 1:17.

13. *One Yet Two: Monastic Tradition East and West,* edited by M. Basil Pennington OCSO, Cistercian Studies series 29 (Kalamazoo: Cistercian Publications, 1976) 166.

14. Denis Ouaillarbourou, Martine Plouvier, F. Placide Vernet, 'Une nouvelle église pour les moines de Cîteaux—1998', *Pour une histoire monumentale de l'abbaye de Cîteaux 1098-1998,* edited by Martine Pouvier, Studia et Documenta 8 (Cîteaux: Commentarii Cistercienses, 1998) 366.

15. D. Ouaillarbourou, 'Une nouvelle église', 368.

16. E. Cazabonne, 'À la rencontre du Soleil: relecture des Sermons de Saint Bernard pour le cycle de la Nativité', *Collectanea Cisterciensa* 58 (1995) 331-344. And 'Access to Inaccessible Light: Bernard's Use of 1 Tm 6:16', *Cistercian Studies Quarterly* 38 (2003) 275–284.

17. Emmanuel Cazabonne, 'Gregory Palamas (1296–1359): Monk, Theologian, and Pastor', *Cistercian Studies Quarterly* 37 (2002) 303–332.

18. On the genres of *florilegium* and century, see Jean Leclercq OSB, *The Love of Learning and the Desire of God: A Study of Monastic Culture.* Translated by Catherine Misrahi (New York: Fordham University Press, 1961) 228–230.

19. See *The Way of a Pilgrim,* translated by R. M. French, edited by Dennis Joseph Billy (Liguori, Missouri: Liguori Publications, 2000) 7.

20. Those Pauline words (Eph 5:8) happen to be Saint Bernard's very last words in Sermon 86 on the Song of Songs, his last sermon on this biblical book: *ut filii, inquit, lucis ambulate. Sancti Bernardi Opera* edited by J. Leclercq and H. M. Rochais (Rome: Editiones Cistercienses, 1958) 2:320, line 10.

Daily Readings for Meditation

Long before the night office began, the man of God was standing at his window, where he watched and prayed while the rest were still asleep. In the dead of the night, he suddenly beheld a flood of light shining down from above more brilliant than the sun, and with it every trace of darkness cleared away. Another remarkable sight followed. According to his own description, the whole world was gathered up before his eyes in what appeared to be a single ray of light.

Keep this well in mind. All creation is bound to appear small to a soul that sees the Creator. Once it beholds a little of his light, it finds all creatures small indeed. The light of holy contemplation enlarges and expands the mind in God until it stands above the world. In fact, the soul that sees him rises even above itself, and as it is drawn upward in his light all its inner powers unfold. Then, when it looks down from above, it sees how small everything is that was beyond its grasp before.

Gregory the Great
Dialogues 2.35

O love, to see you is to be in ecstasy in God. To cling to you is to be joined to God by a nuptial contract. O serenest light of my soul, very brightest morning, ah, break into day in me now and begin so to shine for me that by your light I may see light[1] and that through you my night may be turned into day. By the love of your love, O my dearest morning, let me reckon everything that you are not as if it were nothing and void. Ah! Visit me now in the morning at daybreak that I may suddenly be transformed entirely into you.

Gertrud the Great of Helfta
Spiritual Exercises, 5

[1] *Ps 35:10*

The day will breathe forth life, the night will breathe its last. The night is the devil, night is the angel of Satan, though he may disguise himself as an angel of light.[1] Night is the Antichrist, whom the Lord shall slay with the breath of his mouth and destroy with the brightness of his coming. Is not the Lord the day? Clearly he is the day, bright and throbbing with life. He puts the shadows to flight with the breath of his mouth, and destroys the phantoms with the brightness of his coming.

When the day breathes forth life the shadows truly lie prostrate, for when the fullness of night pervades all things, then no trace of shadows can remain! For when that which is perfect is come, that which is in part shall be done away!

Bernard of Clairvaux
Sermon 72 on the Song of Songs, 5

[1] *2 Cor 11:14*

> *Come to him and be enlightened:*
> *and your faces shall not be confounded.*[1]

Behold, I am approaching you, O consuming fire, my God.
Ah! Devouring me, a speck of dust, in the fiery vigor of
your love, consume me utterly and absorb me into yourself.
Behold, I am approaching you, O my dulcet light. Ah! Let
your face light up over me[2] so that my darkness may become
like noonday in your presence. Behold, I am approaching
you, O most blessed union. Ah! Make me one with you by
the glue of living love.

Gertrud the Great of Helfta
Spiritual Exercises, 4

[1] *Ps 33:6*
[2] *Ps 118:135*

It is to the shepherds watching and keeping the night watches over their flock that the joy of the new light is announced, and for them the Saviour is said to be born. Upon the poor and the toiling, not upon you that are rich and have your consolation, and with it the divinely-denounced woe; the day of sanctification has dawned amid the watches of the night, so that the night is illuminated as the day, or is rather changed into day, since the angel says, not this night, but this day is born to you a Saviour. For the night is passed and the day is at hand, the true Day of true Day, the salvation of God, our Lord Jesus Christ, who is over all things and is himself true God, blessed for evermore. Amen.

Bernard of Clairvaux
Sermon 5 for Christmas Eve, 5

Anyone who now neglects internal holiness shall not be admitted hereafter to the contemplation of majesty; the Sun of glory shall never shine on him on whom the Sun of justice has not risen; nor shall he see the dawn of tomorrow who has not lived in the light of today. For, as the apostle teaches, the same Christ, who of God is made unto us justice today, shall appear as our life tomorrow, when we also shall appear with Him in glory. Today he is born for us as a little one, that man may no more presume to magnify himself upon earth, but that we may rather be converted and become as little children. But tomorrow he will show himself to us as the great Lord and greatly to be praised, so that we also shall be magnified in glory when every man shall have praise from God. For those whom he justifies today, he will magnify tomorrow, and to the consummation of holiness shall succeed the vision of Majesty.

Bernard of Clairvaux
Sermon 5 for Christmas Eve, 3

You fear the Lord of the angels, but love the little child. You fear the Lord of majesty, but love the babe wrapped in swaddling clothes. You fear him reigning in heaven, but love him lying in the manger. But what sign did the shepherds receive? You will find a baby wrapped in swaddling clothes and lying in a manger. This sign meant that he is the Saviour, that he is the Christ, that he is the Lord. But is there anything great about being wrapped in swaddling clothes and lying in a stable? Are other children not wrapped in swaddling clothes? What does this sign mean then? It means a great deal if only we understand it. We do understand it if we do not merely hear these tidings but also have in our hearts the light which appeared with the angels. He appeared with light when these tidings were first proclaimed to make us realize that it is only those who have the spiritual light in their minds who truly hear.

Aelred of Rievaulx
Sermon 3 for the Nativity of the Lord, 37–38

My advice is that you go now to the Word, and he will teach you his ways, so that you will not go astray in your journey and, desiring the good but not recognizing it, wander in a pathless place instead of along the highway. The Word is the light.[1] The unfolding of your words gives light and imparts understanding to children.[2] Happy are you if you too can say, 'Your word is a lamp for my feet and a lantern for my path'.[3] Your soul has received great profit if your will is unswerving and your reason enlightened, willing and recognizing the good. By the first it receives life and by the second vision; for it was dead when it desired evil, and blind when it did not recognize the good.

Bernard of Clairvaux
Sermon 85 on the Song of Songs, 2

[1] *Jn 1:9*
[2] *Ps 118:130*
[3] *Ps 118:105*

When it was night we were incapable of any good, so the Light freely came into the world and took the world by surprise. We were born when it was night, we were brought up in the night, but though composed of clay from beneath, we are also of spittle from above—spittle from the Head, clay from beneath the foot. When mud made of this clay and spittle was smeared on the eyes of the man born blind his eyes were opened. That universal night is past in which all have sinned; it has gone, the Sun is shining, the darkness has so vanished that those who could not work previously have not the least excuse now if they refuse to work in the daylight. As he who is the Day says: 'If I had not come and given them my message', meaning, 'if I had not shone on them they would not have been at fault; as it is, their fault can find no excuse.'[1]

Whoever does not make use of grace given is neglecting the duties of the daylight and is rightly rebuked for idleness.

Isaac of Stella
Sermon 16,13–14

[1] *Jn 15:22*

David says of the Lord that he pitched his tent in the sun, and comes out of his pavilion like a bridegroom. He exulted like a giant to run his race: his going out is from the highest heavens.[1] What a leap he made from the highest heavens to the earth! Indeed I can discover no place, other than the earth, where he would pitch his tent in the sun: that is, where he who dwells in unapproachable light[2] would deign to reveal his presence openly and in the light. For he appeared upon earth and lived among men. Upon earth, I say, in plain sight, which is meant by pitching his tent in the sun, namely, in the body which he was pleased to prepare for himself for this purpose from the Virgin's body, that in it he who is by nature invisible might be seen, and so all mankind should see the salvation of God on his coming in the flesh.

Bernard of Clairvaux
Sermon 53 on the Song of Songs, 7

[1] *Ps 18:6-7*
[2] *1 Tm 6:16*

Our most blessed Lady is a unique castle, since in no other human being is there such humility, in none other such perfect chastity, in none other such surpassing charity. A unique castle, without a doubt; one which the Father fashioned, which the Holy Spirit sanctified, and which the Son entered, one which the whole Trinity uniquely chose for themselves as a lodging.

This is the castle which Jesus entered. He entered with the gate shut and with the gate shut he exited, as the holy Ezekiel had foretold: he brought me round to the gate that faced eastward and it was shut. The east gate is Mary most holy. For the gate which faces east generally receives the brightness of the sun first. So Mary most blessed, who always looked to the east, to the brightness of God, first received within herself the ray, indeed, the whole fullness of the brightness of the true sun, the Son of God, of whom Zachary said: the rising Sun visited us from on high.[1]

Aelred of Rievaulx
Sermon 19 for the Assumption of Saint Mary, 15–16

[1] *Lk 1:78*

We were wholly unable to come near to you, the dawning splendor of light eternal, and yet you came near to us by that same free and innate goodness with which, born from the Father's womb before the daystar,[1] you glimmered so wonderfully in the saints' first splendors. Since you were wisdom, the fashioner of all things, with wonderful and delicate craft you have fashioned a salvation adapted to the blind and sickly. The world did not have the wisdom to know you in the invisible light of your wisdom, so it seemed proper to your honor to enlighten the blind and to cure the sick by means of foolishness. You were a great light hidden in the bosom of your Father; you came forth from your retreat into our market place. You became a great light for the great, and a small lamp for the little ones; you became a lamp not only visible to our eyes but palpable to our touch. In this way you brought news of it to your friend, that it was for him to possess and mount up to it.

John of Forde
Sermon 7 on the Song of Songs, 5

[1] Ps 110:3

You broke forth from the pure womb of the virgin, O purest of lights, and there indeed you set your tabernacle in the sun,[1] but one which you fashioned for yourself as the font of light. Therefore, O blessed light, since you were wisdom, wisely you subdued yourself to the unwise.

Further, because you were truth, you threw your beams into the darkness to dispel the night of our ignorance and to refute the works of darkness. You thundered from the cloud of the flesh, threatening judgment and announcing the kingdom. You glittered in signs and wonders and made it clear that you were our true and sole salvation, taking away our sin.

John of Forde
Sermon 7 on the Song of Songs, 5

[1] *Ps 19:4*

And the Virgin's name was Mary.[1] Let us now say a few words about this name, which means star of the sea and is so becoming to the Virgin Mother. Surely she is very fittingly likened to a star. The star sends forth its ray without harm to itself. In the same way the Virgin brought forth her son with no injury to herself. The ray no more diminishes the star's brightness than does the Son his mother's integrity. She is indeed that noble star risen out of Jacob[2] whose beam enlightens this earthly globe. She it is whose brightness both twinkles in the highest heaven and pierces the pit of hell,[3] and is shed upon earth, warming our hearts far more than our bodies, fostering virtue and cauterizing vice. She, I tell you, is that splendid and wondrous star suspended as by necessity over this great wide sea, radiant with merit and brilliant in example. O you, whoever you are, who feel that in the tidal wave of this world you are nearer to being tossed about among the squalls and gales than treading on dry land, if you do not want to founder in the tempest, do not avert your eyes from the brightness of this star. When the wind of temptation blows up within you, when you strike upon the rock of tribulation, gaze up at this star, call out to Mary. Whether you are being tossed about by the waves of pride or ambition or slander or jealousy, gaze up at this star, call out to Mary. When rage or greed or fleshly desires are battering the skiff of your soul, gaze up at Mary. When the immensity of your sins weighs you down and you are bewildered by the loathsomeness of your conscience, when the terrifying thought of judgment appalls you and you begin to founder in the gulf of sadness and despair, think of Mary. In dangers, in hardships, in every doubt, think of Mary, call out to Mary. Keep her in your mouth, keep her in your heart. Follow the example of her life and you will obtain the favor of her prayer. Following her, you will never go astray. Asking her help, you will never despair. Keeping her in your thoughts, you will never wander away. With your hand in hers, you will never stumble. With her protecting you, you will not be afraid. With her leading you, you will never tire. Her kindness will see you through to the end. Then you will know by your own experience how true it is that the Virgin's name was Mary.

Bernard of Clairvaux
Homily 2 in Praise of the Virgin Mother, 17

[1] *Lk 1:27*
[2] *Nm 24:17*
[3] *Prv 5:5*

The only-begotten Son of God, the Sun of justice, has shown himself amidst the gloom of this place of our banishment as a burning and shining torch, of large and brilliant flame, in order, namely, that all who desire to be illuminated may approach and be united to him so closely as to leave nothing intervening between him and them. For it is our sins that separate between us and God. Therefore, as soon as these are removed, we are placed in contact with the true Light of the world, to be enlightened by and, as it were, made one with it; just as when we want to light an extinguished taper we touch it to another that is burning and shining.

At this great and luminous Star let us then light for ourselves the lamp of knowledge, as the Prophet speaks, before we pass out of the darkness of this world.

Bernard of Clairvaux
Sermon 3 for Christmas Eve, 2

Because of his indescribable kindness, which made him appear on the earth and live among men, the Wisdom of God consented to assume the appearance of toil in the giving of a command and first anointed the eyes of the blind with the clay of his flesh and then ordered light to shine from the darkness; next by degrees he produced from these eyes stars and then, after the stars, created the sun and its rising. So those eyes shone as if fixed in the sky, which is the face of Jesus, and as if they were the noonday sun, and they gave light to the earth. Through them, just as through his own eyes, the Lord looked down from heaven on all who dwell on the earth, taking away the darkness of ungodliness, drying up the clay of wickedness, and through them making known to the world the paths of life.

John of Forde
Sermon 16 on the Song of Songs, 3

O sweet light, O life-giving light, by sending forth your wisdom and truth you instructed our mind; by instilling the light of your holiness and goodness you wonderfully illuminated our heart. In these wonderful ways your lightning has lit up the world,[1] just as you light up every single son of light in the world. This is what can be said about the radiance of the eternal light, that is, the radiance of the beloved, as far as we can understand it, or rather, as far as he gives us to understand.

John of Forde
Sermon 7 on the Song of Songs, 5

[1] *Ps 77:18*

In the morning you shall see the glory of the Lord.[1]

O most desirable morning! O day in the courts of the Lord that is better above thousands, wherein for ever month shall succeed to month and sabbath to sabbath, while the splendor of light and the fervor of charity shall unfold and illumine the loftiest mysteries of God for the contemplation of the blessed! Oh, who shall presume—I do not say, to describe—but even to imagine your glories? Yet, in the meantime, let us strengthen our faith, in order that, if we cannot behold the wonders which are reserved for the life to come, we may at least contemplate something of the marvels accomplished for us on earth.

Bernard of Clairvaux
Sermon 3 for Christmas Eve, 7

[1] *Ex 16:7*

January 6   *His Name is Sunrise*
The Manifestation of Christ

What more God-like could be manifested to human senses than the prodigies which Jesus today exhibited, long before the beginning of his signs? A new-born child cries on earth while in the heavens he creates a new star, so that light may witness to Light, a star to the Sun, and so that kings in the splendor of its rising[1] may be led to the eternal splendor which has also risen up. They come from the sunrise to the true Sunrise, that is to the man whose name is Sunrise.[2] They are led by the star not as a star but as a rational animal, going before them on the journey, coming to a halt at the end of the journey and pointing out as with a finger him whom they sought.

Guerric of Igny
Sermon 2 for the Epiphany, 2

[1] *Is 60:3*
[2] *Zec 6:12*

Arise, Be Enlightened!

Arise, be enlightened, Jerusalem, *for your Light has come.*[1] This present day of lights has been enlightened for us and consecrated by the Light of Light. He had lain hidden and unknown, but today he has vouchsafed to reveal himself to the world for the enlightenment of all nations. For today he revealed himself to the Chaldeans by the sign of a new star, dedicating in them as in first-fruits the faith of all nations.

Arise, be enlightened, Jerusalem, *for your light has come.*[2] The Light indeed had come; he was in the world, and the world was made through him, but the world did not know him.[3] He was born but he was not known, until this day of light began to manifest him.

Arise, you who sit in darkness; look at the light which has risen up in the darkness but is not mastered by the darkness. Draw near to him and be enlightened,[4] in his light you shall see the light;[5] and it will be said to you: You were once darkness, but now you are light in the Lord.[6]

O look upon the eternal Light which has tempered itself to your gaze, so that he who dwells in inaccessible light[7] affords access even to weak and bleary eyes. See the Light in a lamp of earthenware, the Sun in a cloud, God in man, the splendor of glory and brightness of eternal Light[8] in the clay vessel of your flesh.

Guerric of Igny
Sermon *2 for the Epiphany*, 1

[1] *Is 60:1*
[2] *Is 60:1*
[3] *Jn 1:10*
[4] *Ps 33:6*
[5] *Ps 35:10*
[6] *Eph 5:8*
[7] *1 Tm 6:16*
[8] *Ws 7:26*

Arise, be enlightened, Jerusalem, *for your Light, has come.*[1] Blessed is the Light which has come in the name of the Lord, God the Lord, and has shone upon us.[2] In virtue of it this day also, sanctified by the enlightening of the Church, has shone upon us. Thanks be to you, true Light, you that enlighten every man coming into this world,[3] you who for this very purpose have come into this world as a man. Jerusalem has been enlightened, our mother, mother of all those who have deserved to be enlightened, so that she now shines upon all who are in the world. Thanks be to you, true Light, you who have become a lamp to enlighten Jerusalem and to make God's word a lamp for my feet.[4] Thanks be to you, I say, because Jerusalem itself, enlightened, has become a lamp to shine upon all who are in the house[5] of the great Father. For not only has it been enlightened: it has been raised aloft on a candlestick, one all of gold.

Guerric of Igny
Sermon 3 for the Epiphany, 1

[1] *Is 60:1*　　　[4] *Ps 118:105*
[2] *Ps 117:26*　　[5] *Mt 5:15*
[3] *Jn 1:9*

The star which leads us to Jesus is sacred Scripture. Behold our light has already come,[1] because for us and for our salvation God has become man. He was seen on earth and dwelt among men and women, so that, by the might of his word and the example of his life he might enlighten those who are sitting in darkness and direct them into the way of peace.[2] It is no wonder that before the Lord's coming, when they had heard nothing of God, when they did not discern the light of Scripture, the pagans lay prostrate in their sins and in the darkness of their errors. But now lying prostrate in carnal desires and in the darkness of iniquities is a matter for great agitation, for the true light that enlightens every one coming into this world,[3] Christ Jesus, has now come. We cannot have further excuse for our sins, for Christ, who takes away the sins of the world and justifies the wicked, now speaks to us openly. Someone who follows me does not walk in darkness but will have the light of life.[4]

Aelred of Rievaulx
Sermon 4 for the Epiphany, 32–33

[1] *Is 60:1*
[2] *Lk 1:79*
[3] *Jn 1:9*
[4] *Jn 8:12*

O most beautiful Light, O radiance of light eternal, you were like that from the beginning, you were like that, O everlasting loveliness, in those everlasting days of yours, in the years of your eternity! You were like that, O Lord Jesus, wise, true, holy, good, but you were this for yourself and for your beloved Father, who loves you. With you was the beginning on the day of your birth, and you were with him, and you were total joy to him, and so was he to you.

Still, as you were not only light from light,[1] but also the font of brightness, you wanted to reveal this great good and to share it with your creatures. All of a sudden, then, you glowed radiantly forth in those whom you chose as sharers in so great a good.

John of Forde
Sermon 7 on the Song of Songs, 3–4

[1] *Jn 1:5*

There was darkness over the face of the abyss.[1]

The abyss is the soul on account of the vast depths of its nature. The face of the abyss is the mind. There was darkness over the face of the abyss: the darkness of error, the darkness of heathendom, the terrifying darkness of unbelief. But today those who were earth are told to rise up, those who had darkness over the face of their abyss are told to be enlightened. *Let there be light*[2] is the same as *Be enlightened.*[3] When the heathen are enlightened by faith and the knowledge of God, they become light and they hear Paul say: Once you were darkness but now you are light in the Lord.[4]

Aelred of Rievaulx
Sermon 4 for the Epiphany, 13–14

[1] *Gn 1:2*
[2] *Gn 1:3*
[3] *Ps 33:6*
[4] *Eph 5:8*

Let darkness cover the earth and shade the peoples who, when the light came into the world, preferred darkness to light,[1] provided you are enlightened, Jerusalem, heavenly city, you who in every land and people are to bear to God sons of Light whom he will transfer from the power of darkness to the kingdom of his brightness, the true light.[2]

Thank you, Father of lights,[3] who have called us out of darkness into your admirable light.[4] Thanks be to you who bade light shine out of darkness and have kindled a light in our hearts whose shining is to make known your glory as you have revealed it in the features of Jesus Christ.[5] This is the true light, indeed eternal life: that we may know you the one God, and him whom you have sent, Jesus Christ.

> Guerric of Igny
> *Sermon 2 for the Epiphany*, 3

[1] *Jn 3:19*
[2] *Col 1:13*
[3] *Jas 1:17*
[4] *1 Pt 2:9*
[5] *2 Cor 4:6*

The faith of the Magi, although it saw in the babe only what was weak and contemptible, could not however find in that a stumbling-block to prevent them from worshiping God in man and man in God. Without doubt a star out of Jacob[1] had shone in their hearts, the morning Star, I mean, the herald of light which knows no setting, he who from without also had kindled for their hearts a star as a sign of his rising in the morning. What is written in the book of Proverbs can be very aptly understood of these: *The path of the righteous is like the light of dawn, which shines brighter and brighter until full day.*[2] For at first they entered on the path of justice by the light of a dawning star; led by it they advanced to seeing the new rising of early morning Light; and so finally they reached the point where they could contemplate the face of the midday Sun in all the brilliance of its power.

Guerric of Igny
Sermon 2 for the Epiphany, 4

[1] *Nm 24:17*
[2] *Prv 4:18*

For us too stars shine, not one but many, except that the many are one, because they have one heart and one soul, the same faith, a harmonious preaching and a similar life. What are these stars? If you are in doubt, ask Daniel. *They who instruct many unto justice shall shine like stars for all eternity.*[1] Paul also calls those men luminaries who shine in the midst of a wicked and perverse nation[2] and contain the word of life, like splendor borrowed from eternal light, with which they seem to enlighten the night of this world. Therefore when the Lord, the source and origin of light, was disposing the moon and the stars to govern the night,[3] he told them: *You are the light of the world;*[4] and again: *So let your light shine before men that they may see your good works and glorify your Father who is in heaven.*[5] So they shine by their word, they shine by their example, and by these two rays of light they proclaim the rising of eternal Light.

Guerric of Igny
Sermon 2 for the Epiphany, 5

[1] *Dn 12:3*   [4] *Mt 5:14*
[2] *Phil 2:15*   [5] *Mt 5:16*
[3] *Ps 135:9*

From where does the light come to the heathen? Rise up, says the Lord, be enlightened, Jerusalem, for your light has come.[1] This is the whole reason why the holy Church is enlightened, first in the three kings and afterwards in all nations. This is the whole reason, what is said to her through the prophet: Because your light has come. *For a light has arisen in the darkness.*[2] But for whom? Not for the perverse of heart who remain in their darkness, but for the upright of heart who recognize the light and long to adore.

The heart that is empty and a waste is told to rise up, that is, to prepare itself for the things of heaven that are to be desired. And as if to someone who answers, 'I do not see what things of heaven, what things of the spirit I ought to desire', there is added: 'Be enlightened.'

Aelred of Rievaulx
Sermon 4 for the Epiphany, 15–16

[1] *Is 60:1*
[2] *Ps 111:4*

I have seen the day of Jesus, I have seen it and been filled with joy. I have seen the one I long for, I have seen the one I wait for, I have seen the light of my eyes, I have seen the king in his splendor and the beautiful one in his beauty. I have seen him in his glory on the mountain, I have seen him face to face, and yet my life has been preserved. And then, on that day, not only was there a new light shining in my eyes, but even my ears, too, knew joy, pealing in thunderous rapture from the heavens! For the Father, faithful witness in the heavens, bore witness to his Son for me to hear, so that from that day forth, blessed have been my eyes, and blessed, too, my ears! After all this, how joyfully I came down from the mountain, how much more joyfully than once I came down from Mount Sinai! I came down with my face shining with a glory greater than I had ever known, for on it was impressed the glory and splendor of the wonderful light that streams from the face of Jesus. So I returned to the true sons of Israel, to those who rest upon Abraham's bosom, waiting to see what I saw. And I gave them good tidings of great joy, because I looked upon the glory of the Son of God.

John of Forde
Sermon 31 on the Song of Songs, 2

In purely human qualities, he shows himself as lovelier than all the sons of men, and in this appearance too, he shines with wonderful brightness before the eyes of his lovers. For here too, he is very fair, above all the starry constellations,[1] as Scripture says, because all the virtues of the saints draw their brightness from his virtue, shining forth with incomparable splendor. If we ponder on each of the virtues of this man, one by one: his innocence, his gentleness, his humility, his patience, his kindness, justice, compassion, love—the beauty of his appearance is infinite, and there is nothing in all the glories of the saints that can fitly be held up in comparison.

Clearly, we never gaze on that appearance in vain. We never contemplate it without some traces of our ugliness being removed, some treasures of beauty being acquired. Approach it frequently, this is the advice of the Holy Spirit. Come close, and in the light of the appearance of Jesus, be filled with light, be radiantly white and be made new.[2]

John of Forde
Sermon 35 on the Song of Songs, 5

[1] *Ws 7:29*
[2] *Ps 34:6*

Arise, be enlightened, Jerusalem, for your light has come and the glory of the Lord has risen over you.[1] We do not all accept this word, but let the person who can, take it. Someone who does not take it is not condemned, but someone who does not desire it is accused of tepidity. But the person who desires it should know that this light of wisdom is kindled by fervent prayer, just as the light of knowledge is by frequent reading, provided that when you read you use a burning lamp, that is, justice in your deeds and devotion in your sentiments. But do you, Lord, Father of lights,[2] who have sent your only Son, Light born of you, the Light, to enlighten the darkness of mortal men, grant us to come by the way of lights to eternal light, that we may be pleasing to you in the light of the living:[3] You who live and reign for ever and ever. Amen.

Guerric of Igny
Sermon 3 for the Epiphany, 7

[1] *Is 60:1*
[2] *Jas 1:17*
[3] *Ps 53:13*

How shall we explain the worldwide light of faith, swift and flaming in its progress, except by the preaching of Jesus' name? Is it not by the light of this name that God has called us into his wonderful light,[1] that irradiates our darkness and empowers us to see the light?[2] To such as we Paul says: *You were darkness once, but now you are light in the Lord.*[3] This is the name that Paul was commanded to present before kings and pagans and the people of Israel; a name that illumined his native land as he carried it with him like a torch, preaching on all his journeys that the night is almost over, it will be daylight soon—let us give up all the things we prefer to do under cover of the dark; let us arm ourselves and appear in the light. Let us live decently as people do in the daytime.[4] To every eye he was a lamp on its lamp-stand;[5] to every place he brought the good news of Jesus, and him crucified. What a splendor radiated from that light, dazzling the eyes of the crowd, when Peter uttered the name that strengthened the feet and ankles of the cripple, and gave light to many eyes that were spiritually blind![6]

Bernard of Clairvaux
Sermon 15 on the Song of Songs, 6

[1] *1 Pt 2:9*   [4] *Rom 13:12*
[2] *Ps 35:10*   [5] *Mt 5:15*
[3] *Eph 5:8*   [6] *Acts 3:6*

First of all the lamp of faith is lit, so that by it we may work in the night of this world. Therefore it is written in praise of the valiant woman that she rose by night and, working with her hands by day and by night, she did not eat her bread in idleness: her lamp shall not be put out during the night,[1] that is, her faith shall not fail under temptation. By this lamp the works of darkness are not done, rather it is put out when they are done. For he who does evil hates the light;[2] and therefore he extinguishes the lamp of faith, puts behind him mindfulness of God.

Whereas good works, although to avoid vanity they may be done sometimes secretly, are done in light both from within and from without, that is, under the judgment of faith and the witness of God; because they are works of light, lamps burning in the hands of those who do them as they await the coming of the Bridegroom[3] who will bring forth your justice like the light[4] into the sight of men and angels. As the midday sun is bright[5] so will your deeds be bright, because they are done in God, so that the judgment of all may make God bright in you and you in God.

Guerric of Igny
Sermon 3 for the Epiphany, 4

[1] *Prv 31:15*   [4] *Ps 36:6*
[2] *Jn 3:20*   [5] *Is 18:4*
[3] *Lk 12:35*

Let faith be for us like the first day on which we believers are separated from unbelievers, as light from darkness. Let hope be the second day: through it, dwelling in the heavens and through the merits of faith hoping only for things above the heavens, with God urging us on, we are distinguished from those who, relishing what is upon earth and importuning God for only earthly things, flood and ebb like waters under the firmament of heaven. Let temperance dawn on us like the third day on which, while we mortify our bodies on earth and restrain within necessary limits concupiscences of the flesh like the most brackish waters, the parched and waterless soil of our hearts emerges, thirsting for the Lord God. At last, like the light of the fourth day, let prudence burst forth. By prudence let us distinguish, as between day and night, what we should and should not do. With its help let the light of wisdom shine like the splendor of the sun, and let the light of spiritual knowledge, which waxes in some of us or wanes in others, appear like the beauty of the moon. Through prudence also let the devout mind gaze at the examples of our forefathers as at clusters of stars, and through it mark division between days and years, months and hours.

Aelred of Rievaulx
The Mirror of Charity, 1.32.90

Sometimes I hear your Spirit's voice, and, though it is no more than as the whistling of a gentle air that passes me, I understand the message: *Come unto him and be enlightened.*[1] I hear, and I am shaken. Arising as from sleep and shaking off my lethargy, a certain wonder fills me. I open my mouth and I draw in my breath; I stretch my spiritual muscles and rouse them from their sloth. I turn my back on the shades of night in which my conscience lies and come forth to the Sun of Righteousness[2] who is rising now for me. But I am drowsy still, and the eyes of my reason are dazzled when I try to look at him. For they are used to darkness and unaccustomed to the light; and, while both pupils and eyelids tremble and blink at the unwonted brightness, as best I can I wipe the rheum of my long sleep from them with the hand of exercise. If by your gift I find a fount of tears such as is wont to spring up speedily in lowly ground and in the valleys of a contrite soul, I wash the hands with which I work and the face I lift in prayer. Then, as the falcon spreads his wings towards the south to make his feathers grow, I stretch out my two hands to you, O Lord. My soul is as waterless ground in your sight, and as desert land, unwatered and untrodden, I appear before you in your holy place, that I may see your power and your glory. And when I raise to you, O Sun of Righteousness, the eyes of my mind and the perception of my reason, it happens to me as is wont to happen to persons drunk with sleep or of weak eyes. Seeing one thing, they think that they are seeing two or three, until in the process of seeing it dawns upon them that the defect is in their sight, and not in the thing seen.

William of Saint Thierry
Meditation 2.6

[1] *Ps 33:6*
[2] *Mal 4:2*

When the Lord purifies the eye of a man's mind, enabling him to perceive truth, he is indeed giving a blind man his sight. It must be clearly understood, then, that when we speak of purity of heart, we do not mean simply that the heart is to be purified from vices, call them disordered desire or perverted love, but that it must be purified from the fantasies that are absorbed by the corporeal senses and remain in the imagination, for these become an obstruction that prevents our seeing the sun's clear light. They either cut us off from that solar body, the very source of light itself—they are so unlike it—or at least they reduce the sun's brightness.

Isaac of Stella
Sermon 4.3

Suppose that a man had the power to fly into the sky above us. He would have to leave the earth behind, and the waters that are said to be above the earth, and finally those lighter waters that hang in such wondrous fashion and are called clouds. So too the man who raises his mind's eye to see that which is purely incorporeal, must not only rise above every corporeal substance and image of corporeal substance, he must also rise above the whole seething complexity of his own thoughts. Don't let this discourage you! Once you have passed through all these clouds by vigilance of mind and purity of heart, once your every thought is silent, or, rather, left far behind then, at last, there will appear before you a shining cloud, a cloud filled with light,[1] not stormy now nor dense, a cloud of wisdom, not of ignorance.

For there is darkness in light, darkness all the deeper in much light, until finally, when the light reaches the threshold of its own incomprehensibility and enters that unapproachability in which dwells that peace which passes all understanding, it is taken from our eyes so that any further knowledge of the Light is obtained not through speculation but through revelation, just as the apostles gazing heavenward, learned from the men who stood beside them in white garments.[2]

Isaac of Stella
Sermon 4.4–5

[1] *Mt 17:5*
[2] *Acts 1:9-10*

Our heart needs purification, that leaving earth and water far behind, it may ascend into the tranquil region of the reason, there to catch sight of the lowest incorporeal objects. Rising still higher, it reaches the firmament of intelligence, where the second order of the incorporeal comes into view. Finally, it soars into the fiery brightness of understanding, as if onto Mount Tabor, that exceedingly high mountain, and there it sees the third order of the incorporeal, the unseen. There it gazes upon Jesus, Jesus transfigured, glorified, the glory of his flesh making his very garments such as no fuller on earth could make them.[1] But our heart is overwhelmed by the glory of his face, because of that pure form of incomprehensibility, incorporeity and invisibility in which he remains always equal to the Father. Reason, intellect, and understanding fall on their faces.

Isaac of Stella
Sermon 4.9

[1] *Mk 9:2*

Truly, dear friends, just as time itself is punctuated by light and darkness, day and night, so too is man's life, this transient one, passed sometimes in darkness at the midday sun,[1] at other times in light though it be midnight. God did not bid night come from day, but bade light shine out from darkness.[2] Children of this world, children of night and darkness, are born in darkness; yes, and children of the light and of the day have no other birthplace! The apostle not only wrote to the latter, *You are all born to the light, born to the day; you do not belong to the night and its darkness,*[3] but also, *Once you were all darkness; now, in the Lord, you are all daylight.*[4]

So true is this parentage that the children of light are called light, the children of darkness darkness; it is ever a case of, 'Like father, like son'. It follows that unbelief is night and faith is day; sin is night, virtue is day; ignorance is darkness, while wisdom is light; hatred and love are as darkness and light; the devil is darkness, God is light,[5] which explains why Adam is darkness and Christ is light. To draw this list to a close: a guilty conscience and delight in sin are night and deep darkness; a good conscience and love of virtue are dazzling daylight. Worldly wisdom and life are darkness; spiritual wisdom and life are daylight.

Isaac of Stella
Sermon 16.8-9

[1] *Dt 28:29*   [4] *Eph 5:8*
[2] *2 Cor 4:6*   [5] *1 Jn 1:5*
[3] *1 Thes 5:5*

My soul is a trouble to me, sings the seer, and therefore he began to be mindful of God, as of the daylight.[1] For God is all light, and in him alone no darkness can find any place.[2] Though the holy angels find their morning in him, yet they stumble in the evening they find in themselves; this evening of theirs and the morning of God go to make that one, first day.[3] God alone finds the light of day in himself, and once he begins thanks to his purely gratuitous grace to shine in rational minds, he creates morning and separates light from darkness.[4]

Grace, then, is the dawn of the spiritual day; it not only anticipates reason, it turns it from itself to God and leads it from the darkness of ignorance or of weakness and even of ill-will, into the daylight of wisdom, virtue and justice, the day, in other words, of Christ our Lord.

Isaac of Stella
Sermon 17.5–6

[1] *Ps 41:7*
[2] *1 Jn 1:5*
[3] *Gn 1:5*
[4] *Gn 1:4*

As an eye capable of seeing yet ever needing the light that enables it actually to see, and as an ear fit for hearing and hearing only what sound comes from outside itself, neither of these is sufficient of itself: so man's mind, though the initial gift of creating grace makes it capable of seeing God-given light always, needs a ray of light from above in order to really attain vision. The eye does not see the sun save in the light of the sun; created minds cannot have sight of the true divine sun and Light except in the light he bestows. *In your light*, says the prophet, *shall we see light.*[1]

The Word that lights up our minds is just like a ray of sunlight that enables us to see the sun, which otherwise we could not see, a ray that without cutting itself off from the sun comes from the sun and gives us sight of it. While still dwelling in God, he comes forth from him and enables us first to see the splendor that makes it possible for us to see anything at all and then shows us the Father who neither forsakes nor is forsaken by his Son.

Isaac of Stella
Sermon 26.6-7

[1] *Ps 35:10*

Our bodily eyes perceive the light that streams from the sun and in that light see everything else. Following the sun's rays back to their source, we can catch sight of the sun itself, fount and cause of the brightness through which it shows itself by means of its own gift and native benefit. Our minds first glimpse the radiance of unapproachable Light,[1] indispensable condition of their seeing at all, and that Light lifts them up, shows them where it came from, and unveils the course of its origin, something it could by no means do unless it came forth from there.

The Son comes out to bestow light and does so precisely because he comes from the Father. The privilege he has of his nature is one thing, his natural source another. He owes both the brightness through which he enlightens and the enlightenment that comes of his splendor to the unique source of all light. This is not to say that he is first Light, then radiance, thirdly enlightening, but that is because he is Light, his brightness is ever, as far as his being is concerned, a source of enlightenment, though it is not sufficient to enlighten any particular object immediately.

Isaac of Stella
Sermon 26.8–9

[1] *1 Tm 6:16*

In the highest heaven is his glory,[1] supremely radiant and sublime. There love burns bright and understanding is vigorous, there goodwill is ever eager and memory wide-awake. There no anxiety distracts, no difficulty presses, no fear disturbs, no hope seduces, but everything works together to praise and take delight in the Son of God. There day utters speech to day,[2] and I long to utter it to you, but this is a matter too high for me, and beyond all your capacities. Yet on that day of triumph in the height of heaven, when everyone is both a son of day[3] and a day, day truly utters speech to day, one day crying aloud to another, *In the beginning was the Word* and *the Word was made flesh*.[4]

In short, there the appearance of my beloved diffuses itself throughout that whole sphere of light, pouring itself abroad without restraint, and thus wrests every eye impetuously to itself while it powerfully transforms every face into the likeness of its own brilliance.

John of Forde
Sermon 34 on the Song of Songs, 2

[1] *Lk 2:14*
[2] *Ps 19:2*
[3] *1 Thes 5:5*
[4] *Jn 1:1, 1:14*

Glorious among lilies is truth, radiant to behold, and very fragrant; its radiance and the radiance of the eternal Light,[1] the splendor and the figure of God's substance.[2] It is clearly a lily which our earth brought forth for a new benediction, and prepared before the face of all people, alight to lighten the Gentiles.[3] As long as the earth lay under a curse, it brought forth thorns and thistles. But now truth has sprung from the earth by the Lord's blessing, the flower of the field and the lily of the valley. Recognize the lily by its radiance, which shone in the night for the shepherds when it first bloomed, for the Gospel says that the angel of the Lord stood before them and the brightness of the Lord shone round about them.[4] Truly the Lord's radiance, because it was not that of an angel, but that of the lily. The angel was present, certainly, but it was the lily which shone, even from Bethlehem. Recognize the lily by its fragrance, by which it made itself known to the Magi when they were far away. The star did indeed appear, but the Wise Men would not have followed it had they not been drawn by the secret sweetness of the lily's bloom. Truth is indeed a lily whose fragrance awakens faith, whose splendor enlightens the mind.

Bernard of Clairvaux
Sermon 70 on the Song of Songs, 5

[1] *Ws 7:26*   [3] *Lk 2:31-32*
[2] *Heb 1:3*   [4] *Lk 2:9*

Perhaps the Bridegroom called himself a lily because he is wholly surrounded by lilies, and all the events of his life are lilies: his conception, birth, way of life, teaching, the miracles he did, the sacraments he ordained, his passion and death, his resurrection and ascension. Which of these are not radiant and sweetly fragrant? At his conception there streamed from the fullness of the overshadowing spirit a shaft of heavenly brightness so blinding that not even the holy Virgin could have endured it had not the power of the Spirit given her shade. His birth radiated through the undefiled purity of his mother; his life was aflame with innocence, his teaching with truth, his miracles with purity of heart, his sacraments with the hidden power of his goodness; his passion shone with his acceptance of suffering, his death with the freedom he had to avoid death, his resurrection with the radiance which gave fortitude to the martyrs, his ascension with the glory of promises fulfilled.

Bernard of Clairvaux
Sermon 70 on the Song of Songs, 7

The dawn, and a quite clouded one at that, was the whole life of Christ upon earth, which remained obscure until he died and rose again, to put the dawn to flight by the clearer light of his glorious presence. With the coming of sunrise, night was swallowed up in victory.[1] And so we are told that very early on the Sunday morning, just after sunrise, they came to the tomb. Surely it was morning when the sun had risen. But the resurrection endowed it with a new beauty, with a more serene light than usual, because even though we once knew him according to the flesh, we know him thus no longer. The prophet wrote: *He is robed in majesty; the Lord is robed, he is girded with strength,*[2] because he shook off the flesh's frailties like cloudlets and put on the robe of glory. Since then the Sun is risen indeed, and has gradually poured down its rays over the earth;[3] its light has begun to appear increasingly clearer, its warmth to be more perceptible.

Bernard of Clairvaux
Sermon 33 on the Song of Songs, 6

[1] *1 Cor 15:54*
[2] *Ps 93:1*
[3] *Hab 3:11*

When you ask, how my beloved is more than another beloved, I have a ready answer at hand. In the same way as the Father is lovely and desirable, just so is his only-begotten Son. Radiant from the radiant, red from the ruddy. Seeing that my beloved is truly a fire, he shines and burns exceedingly. But he does this as one whom the Father loves and he is in turn loved totally with an equal charity, for the Father is the source of light and heat to his loved and loving only Son. So together they are one light and one heat, and light as being wisdom, truth, holiness, goodness.

John of Forde
Sermon 7 on the Song of Songs, 3

The Lord's command is full of light, it enlightens the eyes,[1] and with those eyes you will be able afterwards to look on the Light itself, when you have grown accustomed to living in the light of its rays, that is, in the fulfillment of the commandments.

Light is pleasant, as Solomon says, *and the eyes delight in beholding the sun*.[2] Pleasant indeed and delightful, but for those who can bear it. It fosters healthy eyes, but it tortures weak eyes. And whose sight is so healthy and so keen that it is not enfeebled by the vision of that invisible Sun? Who can search out majesty and not be overwhelmed by its glory? Your brightness, Lord, is too wonderful for me, both on its own account and on my account; for it is strengthened against me, while my gaze is weakened in me. I am no longer able to bear it[3] as I could in Adam. Perhaps I may be able to bear the brightness of stars, although I cannot bear the Sun itself.

Guerric of Igny
Sermon 2 for the Epiphany, 6

[1] *Ps 18:9*
[2] *Si 11:7*
[3] *Ps 138:6*

Look up to heaven's luminaries, raise your eyes to the mountains from where help will come to you if you revere him who dwells in the heavens, that is, in the mountains themselves. From the mountains, I mean, help will come to you, for a Light that is beyond your reach[1] enlightens wonderfully from the eternal mountains.[2] The mountains have received a Light for the people[3] and from them it will come down upon the valleys and fields that lie beneath them. So I say this: to attend to those who are enlightened is an excellent beginning of enlightenment and one suited to our weakness. The straightest way to finding Jesus is to follow the guiding light of the fathers who have gone before us. The path of the just has been made straight, the way of the just is straight to walk on. He who follows the just man does not walk in darkness but will have the light of life[4] and not only see it. He will see it for the comforting of his present life, he will have it to possess as an eternal inheritance.

Guerric of Igny
Sermon 2 for the Epiphany, 7

[1] *1 Tm 6:16*

[2] *Ps 75:5*

[3] *Ps 71:3*

[4] *Jn 8:12*

Light is sweet, says Solomon, and *it is pleasant to behold the sun with eyes.*[1] How sweeter to behold the light of the sun? The spouse is himself light,[2] and his whole face shines like the sun, yet in the eyes of this sun the force of his beauty is exceptional, it demands our admiration, and there is a kind of perpetual splendor of light, glittering with grace. In Daniel, the eyes of the son of man are compared to flames of fire,[3] and they are described by Jacob as more beautiful than wine. Well then, if they are a flame of fire, why do I not draw near them to warm myself?

John of Forde
Sermon 18 on the Song of Songs, 1

[1] *Qo 11:7*
[2] *Mt 17:2*
[3] *Rv 1:14*

O sweetness ever ancient and ever new, to enjoy you for eternity is to be constantly aroused to desire, to possess you completely is to be constantly stirred to new longings. O morning splendor of eternal brightness, how joyfully you irradiate those who enjoy you! You are always with them, and yet you are always breaking upon their eyes like the morning splendor of the rising sun. Truly, one day within your courts is better than a thousand elsewhere, because there the noontide brightness of your face is equally the brightness of early dawn. It is noontide because of the all-embracing finality of its immense radiance, but early morning because of its lovely freshness. What an amazing miracle of happiness this is: complete satisfaction that is never endangered, because desire is always stretching ahead of it!

John of Forde
Sermon 38 on the Song of Songs, 5

When you had brought me, quite undeserving, up against that most desirable face which was manifesting the treasures of all blessedness, as described above, I felt light entering through my own eyes, a light which came from your deifying eyes, a light beyond price, bringer of sweetness, which penetrated all my inner being and seemed to produce an extraordinarily supernatural effect in all my limbs. First it seemed to empty my bones of their marrow; then, too, the bones themselves and my flesh melted away into nothingness, so much so that my whole being felt as if it were nothing other than that divine brightness which, in an indescribably delightful manner, engaged in play within itself and showed my soul the priceless pleasure of serenity.

Gertrud the Great of Helfta
The Herald of God's Loving-kindness, 2.21.3

Do you blow for us on the trumpet, good Jesus, at the new moon, at the festival of our solemnity? Truly it is a festival, when you reveal your divine Majesty. Nothing is more festal but nothing is briefer. A day I call it; it is but an hour, an hour truly festal and truly solemn. Reveal in us, good Jesus, some hours of that eternal day.[1] You will at once turn from night into day anyone to whom you reveal the word of your light, for you are eternal day. Flash upon us such lightning as this.[2] Anyone on whom your lightning flashes becomes a flash of lightning. Anyone on whom you shed a ray of your light, you make like yourself. 'We shall be like him', says John, 'when he appears.'

Gilbert of Hoyland
Sermon 18 on the Song of Songs, 5

[1] *Ps 18:3*

[2] *Ps 143:6*

I beseech you, show me where you pasture your flock, where you make it lie down at noon, that is, the whole day long: for that noon is a day that knows no evening. Consequently, a day in your courts is better than a thousand elsewhere, because its sun never sets. But perhaps it had a sunrise, when that sanctified day first dawned upon us through the tender mercy of our God, in which the Rising Sun visited us from heaven.[1] Truly then we received your mercy, O God, in the midst of your temple, when, as you rose out of the shadow of death, the morning light shone over us,[2] and in the dawn we saw the glory of God.[3] How many prophets and kings desired to see this, and did not see it! Why should this have been unless because it was night, and that long-awaited dawn on which mercy had been promised had not yet come?

Bernard of Clairvaux
Sermon 33 on the Song of Songs, 4

[1] *Lk 1:78*
[2] *Is 9:2*
[3] *Ex 16:7*

Though the Word is seen here below, it is in the form that seems good to him, not as he is. For example, take that mighty source of light, I speak of that sun which you see day after day; yet you do not see it as it is, but according as it lights up the air, or a mountain, or a wall. Nor could you see even to this extent if the light of your body, the eye,[1] because of its natural steadiness and clearness, did not bear some degree of likeness to that light in the heavens. Since all the other members of the body lack this likeness, they are incapable of seeing the light. Even the eye itself, when troubled, cannot approach the light, because it has lost that likeness. Just as the troubled eye, then, cannot gaze on the peaceful sun because of its unlikeness, so the peaceful eye can behold it with some efficacy because of a certain likeness. If indeed it were wholly equal to it in purity, with completely clear vision it would see it as it is, because of the complete likeness. And so when you are enlightened you can see even now the Sun of Justice[2] that enlightens every man who comes into this world,[3] according to the degree of the light he gives, by which you are made somehow like him;

but see him as he is you cannot, because not yet perfectly like him. That is why the psalmist says: *Come to him and be enlightened, and your faces shall never be ashamed.*[4] That is very true, provided we are enlightened as much as we need, so that with our unveiled faces contemplating the glory of God, all grow brighter and brighter as we are turned into the same image, as by the spirit of the Lord.[5]

Bernard of Clairvaux
Sermon 31 on the Song of Songs, 2

[1] *Mt 6:22*   [4] *Ps 33:6*
[2] *Mal 4:2*   [5] *2 Cor 3:18*
[3] *Jn 1:9*

That the faith is shadowy is a blessing, it tempers the light to the eye's weakness and prepares the eye for the light; for it is written: *He cleansed their hearts by faith.*[1] Faith therefore does not quench the light but protects it. Whatever it may be that the angel sees, is preserved for me by the shadow of faith, stored up in its trusty breast, until it be revealed in due time. If you cannot yet grasp the naked truth is it not worthwhile to possess it wrapped in a veil? Our Lord's Mother herself lived in the shadow of faith, for she was told: *Blessed are you who believed.*[2] Even the body of Christ was a shadow for her, as implied in the words: *The power of the Most High will cover you with its shadow.*[3] That is no mean shadow which is formed by the power of the Most High. Assuredly there was power in the flesh of Christ that overshadowed the Virgin, since by means of the envelope of his vivifying body she was able to bear his majestic presence, and endure the unapproachable light,[4] a thing impossible to mortal woman.

Bernard of Clairvaux
Sermon 31 on the Song of Songs, 9

[1] *Acts 15:9*
[2] *Lk 1:45*
[3] *Lk 1:35*
[4] *1 Tm 6:16*

In this present time, every single blessing that comes to us from the hand of Jesus falls short of perfection. Otherwise we might perhaps pride ourselves, as if we had already arrived or were already perfect, instead of straining forward, eager to lay hold of perfection one way or another. If we compare our vision in this life, however clear it is, to the sight of that eternal light, in which light is seen in light[1] by the blessed eyes of those in heaven, what is it but cloud and blindness?

John of Forde
Sermon 19 on the Song of Songs, 5

[1] *Ps 35:10*

According to the faith of the holy Fathers, it is a true profession of faith, a true assertion, a true declaration, that God is three and one, and not one alone; and in a certain way our own reason can offer support to this faith. *God dwells in inaccessible light,*[1] but because he has no wish to be totally unknown and, as a consequence of being unknown, also unloved, he therefore shines with a sort of light, albeit faint, in our hearts. To this extent he reveals himself to us more clearly and shows us his nature, and it is this which helps us to come to a better knowledge of his nature, which, according to the little knowledge given to us, we should love with all our heart, all our soul, and all our strength. God, however, is charity, and, as the apostle says, his charity is poured forth in our hearts through the Holy Spirit who is given to us. This charity is in us by grace and reveals to us in a certain way the nature of that incomprehensible charity which is God himself, whose nature is charity or generosity; and by a sort of inward feeling of charity itself, it indicates to our innermost being that the nature of charity is to love and to wish to be loved.

Baldwin of Forde
Spiritual Tractate 15

[1] *1 Tm 6:16*

The light of gold is neither fed from one source or diminished from another, but has within itself an everlasting source and a power of shining with a glorious natural splendor. Externally it shines out to others, but nonetheless internally it shines for itself. In these qualities, is not the image of light-giving charity mirrored with great brightness? For charity, radiant in the witness of her own conscience, neither rests on the praise of others nor loses any of her peculiar glory through their censure. Although that which shows on the outside is bright, much brighter still is that which lies within, certainly keeping some little light for the world without, but retaining a great deal for its own inner illumination.

John of Forde
Sermon 11 on the Song of Songs, 3

You are wholly beautiful, my love.[1]

How is she not wholly beautiful, when she is compared with beauty and wholly compared with all beauty? How is she not wholly beautiful, when into her flows the limitless brightness of eternal light?[2] Truly she is wholly beautiful and surpassing beautiful, when into her at full tide pours all the beauty of the Lord. Yes, his beauty is exalted above the stars but the mirror of his beauty is in his bride. His mirror, we read, is in the clouds of heaven.[3] As long as the bride is a cloud of heaven, a cloud bright and airy, as it were, approaching and enfolding the Sun, so long does the splendor only of the Sun reflect in her and she remains the mirror of his beauty.

Gilbert of Hoyland
Sermon 29 on the Song of Songs, 1

[1] *Sg 4:7*
[2] *Ws 7:26*
[3] *Ex 16:10; Rv 14:14*

Clearly the bride is a cloud because she enjoys the lightness of spiritual affection and the light of understanding. As long as the spiritual soul by the practice of prayer and contemplation is poised on high like a bright and airy cloud, it is all the while wholly beautiful because it is wholly beloved, and without blemish because it has been changed into the color of fervent charity. At the hour of prayer the Bridegroom presents the bride to himself in splendor without blemish or wrinkle, cleansing her not so much in his blood as in his light. How is she not wholly beautiful, in whom the splendor of divine beauty is so clearly expressed? What soul will you show me, which you would dare to define as wholly beautiful, save at this hour alone, when by the ardor of love it is rather dyed than robed in the splendor of the Bridegroom?

Gilbert of Hoyland
Sermon 29 on the Song of Songs, 2

The Lord kindly said, 'By the authority of my divine nature, accept full remission for all your sins and omissions'. Immediately Gertrud saw her soul shining in snowy brightness, free from every spot. Then, after some days, when she came to herself and found her soul still shining with the same brightness that she had known before, she began to fear that she was deceived in such a display of her soul's innocence. For she thought that certainly the purity which had earlier been revealed, even if it had been genuine, nonetheless seemed somewhat clouded as a result of her continual lapses into omissions and frivolity which she had quite often committed from human weakness. The Lord kindly comforted her sense of desolation with these words: 'Do I not keep for myself a greater power than I have conferred on my creatures? For I have endowed the material sun with such power that, if a white cloth has become stained, the stain suddenly vanishes as a result of the power of the sun's heat and intensity and the cloth is restored to an even brighter whiteness than before. How much more will I be able to preserve a soul at which I, the sun's creator, have directed the glance of my mercy, undefiled from every speck of sin or omission? For I purify every stain in it by the force of my white-hot love'.

Gertrud the Great of Helfta
The Herald of God's Loving-kindness, 3.11.1

O sun of righteousness,[1] in making the light of your face[2] and the splendor of your truth to shine before the eyes of all, you invite your bride, whoever she may be: 'Show me your face, my sister!' Forthwith the soul of goodwill, the soul that has received the news of peace from heaven, the man who is Christ's brother and whose soul is called his sister, and is in truth, this soul longs to appear before you in your holy place just as she is, and in your light see light.[3] If she is a sinner, she shows you the face of her misery, and seeks for the face of your mercy. If she is holy, she runs to meet you with the face of her righteousness, and finds in you a face resembling her own; for you love all righteousness, O righteous Lord.

William of Saint Thierry
Meditation 8.1

[1] *Mal 4:2*
[2] *Ps 4:7*
[3] *Ps 35:10*

In receiving the white robe, say: 'Ah Jesus, sun of justice, make me clothe myself with you so that I may be able to live according to your will. Make me, under your guidance, preserve my robe of baptismal innocence white, holy, and spotless, and present it undefiled before your tribunal, so that I may have it for eternal life. Amen.'

In receiving the light, you will pray for inner enlightenment: 'Ah Jesus, inextinguishable light, kindle the burning lamp of your charity within me inextinguishably, and teach me to guard my baptism without blame. Then, when called, I come to your nuptials, being prepared I may deserve to enter into the delights of eternal life to see you, the true light,[1] and the mellifluous face of your divinity. Amen.'

Gertrud the Great of Helfta
Spiritual Exercises, 1

[1] *Ps 35:10*

Seek your Beloved each and every night. Why do I say each and every night? Throughout every single livelong night persevere throughout this task. Do not pause and do not rest until your Beloved rises like the dawn and is enkindled for you like a wedding-torch.[1] Then you can sing the verse of Saint Paul: *the night is far gone, the day is at hand*, although his next verse, *let us then cast off the works of darkness*,[2] cannot be applied to a night such as this. For this night knows not the works of darkness, but rather holds a torch for those who persevere in the race in quest of the Beloved. Good indeed is the night when you are hidden from the riot and the assault of fantasies. And though you are not yet hidden in the shelter of your Beloved's presence, still it is good that from you is concealed the ostentatious presence of vain and carnal thoughts. Night falls that you may not notice, may not see that presence. Still in this night your lamp will not be extinguished that you may seek your Beloved.

Gilbert of Hoyland
Sermon 1 on the Song of Songs, 6

[1] *Is 62:1*
[2] *Rom 13:12*

When beauty and brightness have filled the inmost part of the heart, it must become outwardly visible, and not be like a lamp hidden under a bushel,[1] but be a light shining in darkness,[2] which cannot be hidden. It shines out, and by the brightness of its rays it makes the body a mirror of the mind, spreading through the limbs and senses so that every action, every word, look, movement and even laugh (if there should be laughter) radiates gravity and honor. So when the movements of the limbs and senses, its gestures and habits, are seen to be resolute, pure, restrained, free from all presumption and license, with no sign of triviality and idleness, but given to just dealing, zealous in piety, then the beauty of the soul will be seen openly.

Happy the mind which has clothed itself in the beauty of holiness and the brightness of innocence, by which it manifests its glorious likeness, not to the world but to the Word, of whom we read that he is the brightness of eternal life,[3] the splendor and image of the being of God.[4]

Bernard of Clairvaux
Sermon 85 on the Song of Songs, 11

[1] *Mt 5:15*
[2] *Jn 1:5*
[3] *Ws 7:26*
[4] *Heb 1:3*

On the day of glory, stars will unfold their light in the splendor of the saints and shine to the Lord with gladness, but if you compare a star to the sun, how small is it? It is true that star differs from star in brightness,[1] but this is before the sun appears. Once the sun has risen, all the stars soon go into hiding, yielding their light to the sun as if confessing that the sun alone gives light, and in his sight all shining things are dim.

Well, therefore, does the bride, clinging with longing to the face of her sun; well and wisely does she say: 'My beloved is all radiant.[2] All others derive their radiance from him, and in comparison with him they are hardly radiant at all. He himself is whiter than milk, brighter than the lily, purer than snow, more lucent than the light. He is distinguished among thousands, and from him to his whole church emanates all the radiance there is.

John of Forde
Sermon 3 on the Song of Songs, 5

[1] *1 Cor 15:41*
[2] *Sg 5:10*

Blessed is the man to whom it can be said: *We will run after you in the odor of your ointments.*[1] It is as if to say: 'We will run in the rays of your light', which is the same as 'We go forward by the example of your life and works'. The sweet odor of the saints is their light. How many sinners ran to repent through the example of Saint John! He gave both light and a sweet odor by the good report of his life and by his virtues. He was a burning and shining light set up on high, as if on a sort of candlestick of virtues, scattering on all sides light and a most sweet odor. I want you to be like Saint John. Let your light shine before men, yet so as to burn before God as well, so that men may say of you: He was a burning and shining light. For your own good it is necessary that you should burn, and for the good of those who look to you it is necessary that you should shine. He shines well who is lit by his own fire. Those who do not shine with their own light, shine as hypocrites with a borrowed light, not being on fire themselves. Of the two it were better to burn without shining than to shine without burning.

Bernard of Clairvaux
Letter 505[*]

[1] *Sg 1:3*

[*] *Letter 115 in the Bruno Scott James translation*

Look up into heaven, for your true home is in heaven. Look up and direct the eyes of your mind at least on the brilliance of the stars, if you are not able yet to gaze upon the sun's disk. Admire the splendor of the saints, imitate their faith, emulate their holiness. Those stars blaze like a flame and show clearly that the Light of lights has risen. They lead to the cradle of the new King, to the bedchamber of the Virgin Mother, faith's inviolable mystery, indeed they lead to the temple of the King, to the sanctuary of God the Father, faith's reward that surpasses all understanding. In the meantime however, while we are not able to search out the wisdom of God which is hidden in mystery or to contemplate the majesty which is to be our reward, let us be content to wonder at the brightness of the saints.

Guerric of Igny
Sermon 2 for the Epiphany, 6

Lord, though you have made the darkness of our ignorance and human blindness the secret place that hides your face from us, nevertheless your pavilion is round about you, and some of your saints undoubtedly were full of light. They glowed and they gave light,[1] because they lived so close to your light and your fire. By word and example they kindled and enlightened others, and they declared to us the solemn joy of this supreme knowledge of you, for which we look hereafter, when we shall see you as you are, and face to face. Meanwhile, through them the lightnings of your truth have illumined the world, and flashes have shone forth[2] that rejoice those whose eyes are sound; although they trouble and perturb those who love darkness rather than light.[3]

For this manifestation of your truth, through whomsoever it comes, is like your sun that you make to shine on the just and the unjust alike.[4] The sun, while ever retaining the purity of its own nature, nevertheless makes use of the substances of doings as it finds them. It dries up mud and melts wax. It illumines every eye, whether sighted or blind,

but with different effect; the seeing eye sees more when illumined, the blind continues in its blindness. So, too, it was
when you, God's Wisdom and Truth's Light, by whom all
things were made, came into the world. You enlightened
every man coming into the world, but the darkness did
not embrace you. But to as many as received you and the
light of your truth you gave the power to become the sons
of God.[5]

William of Saint Thierry
Meditation 7.8-9

[1] *Ps 76:19*   [4] *Mt 5:45*
[2] *Jn 5:35*   [5] *Jn 1:5ff*
[3] *Jn 3:19*

Look well at the likeness to these things in our visible light, about which Light itself said: *Let there be light, and there was light.*[1] In a certain manner of its own, that light also illumines the blind and teaches man wisdom, stripping away the darkness of blindness and ignorance in which night had overwhelmed and enveloped him. By the sudden dazzling of its brightness it drives darkness away and lays bare its works, showing up all their falsity. Into that light nothing defiled gains entrance,[2] but it has kept itself immaculate. Finally, it shines equally on the good and the bad, and gives itself freely to both.

John of Forde
Sermon 7 on the Song of Songs, 3

[1] *Gn 1:3*
[2] *Ws 7:23*

It would have been useless for you to show signs and wonders to us exteriorly, had you not also shone interiorly. Since you were holiness, you took great delight in showing your mercy towards us. You filled us with your fear, through which you make us holy, turning us away from our darkness and drawing us compassionately to you, the true light. And finally, since you were goodness, so that you might garb in honor those who had put on the livery of confession, and we might walk becomingly as in the day,[1] you wrapped us around in the light of your justice. You gave us goodness, infusing the spirit of your grace, and our earth has given its fruit.

John of Forde
Sermon 7 on the Song of Songs, 5

[1] *Rom 13:13*

The prophet was told to hide in the hollowed ground. Why? Because without facial beauty he is not fit to be seen. He will not be fit to be seen as long as he is not equipped for seeing. But when by dwelling in the hollow in the ground he will so have succeeded in healing his inward vision that he can gaze on the glory of God with unveiled face, then at last, pleasing both in voice and face, he will confidently proclaim what he sees. The face that can focus on the brightness of God must of necessity be pleasing. Nor could it accomplish this unless it were itself bright and pure, transformed into the very image of the brightness it beholds. Otherwise it would recoil through sheer unlikeness, driven back by the unaccustomed splendor. When a pure soul can therefore gaze on the pure truth, the Bridegroom himself will want to look on his face, and then to hear his voice.

Bernard of Clairvaux
Sermon 62 on the Song of Songs, 7

When fire has consumed every stain of sin and the rust of evil habits, when the conscience has been cleansed and tranquillized and there follows an immediate and unaccustomed expansion of the mind, an infusion of light that illuminates the intellect to understand Scripture and comprehend the mysteries—the first given for our own satisfaction, the second for the instruction of our neighbors—all this undoubtedly means that his eye beholds you, nurturing your uprightness as a light and your integrity as the noonday,[1] as Isaiah says: *Your light shall break forth as the dawn,*[2] and so on. But as long as this mere crumbling wall of the body stands, this ray of intense brightness will pour itself in not through open doors but through chinks and crevices. You are wrong if you hope otherwise, no matter how great your purity of heart, because the greatest of contemplatives, Paul, says: *Now we see only in a riddle and in a mirror, but then we shall see face to face.*[3]

Bernard of Clairvaux
Sermon 57 on the Song of Songs, 8

[1] *Ps 36:6*

[2] *Is 58:8*

[3] *1 Cor 13:12*

The Light of Contemplation
and of Good Works

The mind accustomed to quietude receives consolation from good works rooted in a sincere faith whenever, as often happens, the light of contemplation is withdrawn. For who can enjoy the light of contemplation—I do not say continually but even for long—while she remains in the body? But, as I said, as often as she falls away from contemplation she takes refuge in action, from which she will surely return to the former state as from an adjoining place, with greater intimacy, since these two are comrades and live together: for Martha is sister to Mary. And though she loses the light of contemplation, she does not permit herself to fall into the darkness of sin or the idleness of sloth, but holds herself within the light of good works. And that you may know that good works are light Christ said: *Let your light shine before men;*[1] and there is no doubt that this was said about works that men could see with their eyes.

Bernard of Clairvaux
Sermon 51 on the Song of Songs, 2

[1] *Mt 5:16*

Every just man, every holy man in the Church, for all that he is glad to be enlightened, sees that to a great extent he is still in darkness, and he is saddened by this. Of necessity therefore, although he is enlightened, he asks to be enlightened still more. For the more his lamp is enlightened, the more truly is his darkness revealed to him by the lamp itself. Do not immediately consider as opposed to this the words of incarnate Truth in the gospel: *The lamp of your body is your eye. If your eye is clear your whole body will be lit up.*[1] For it does not follow that because the whole of our activity is lit up by the eye of a pure intention all the darkness of our mistaken opinions and ignorant views is immediately enlightened. The measure of our enlightenment is still this, that the man who is able to know his own inadequacy and recognize what is lacking to him is to be judged as having made great progress towards the light of truth. Hence it is that among the wise men of this world whose disquisitions on the subject of knowledge are the most marked by sobriety the first degree of knowledge is reckoned as knowing one's own ignorance.

Guerric of Igny
Sermon 3 for the Epiphany, 1

[1] *Mt 6:22*

Ida took to demanding of the Almighty that he sweep away the gloomy cloud and again flood her mental dungeon with his daylight. And so? Barely were the words out, barely had she bestirred herself to the effort of making this demand, when, behold, both women looked up the heavens opened; then a great flash bounded down like lightning, gushing over God's venerable servant to bathe her, inside and out, and drench her in its beams, as does the sun. Lit up with so cheery a flood from on high, Ida's mind and affections now replenished themselves until her mood became as of one drunken with boundless spiritual sweetness, as of one conducted to the wine cellar to drink her fill.

She later explained that it had been with her bodily eyes that she had seen all this, and that the upper region of the sky from which the brightness had originated had been split open as along two bands or sashes.

The Life of Ida of Louvain, 1.26

After Ida had already spent some part of the night before the icon of the glorious Mother of God, pounding upon earth with her knees and upon heaven with her tears, and had so offered to the Almighty the incense of praise and thanksgiving as a sweet-smelling odor from the altar of her heart, behold her sister, near at hand all this time, now trained her gaze upon her and saw her and her whole body bathed all over with a light so bright as to gleam like some unearthly substance, like something for only Angels to look upon, sparkling with such beams that her own eyes recoiled.

Not only could the sister not look on her, but she actually had to drop to the floor on her face and howl that she had been blinded. Thus she filled that whole church with her unrestrained shouts and her terrified bellowings and screams. For so great had been the impact of that brightness, as she herself later reported, that her eyesight had been blackened out and she had been unable to see even her own hands, until, a while later, when the forced recoiling had worn off, the focus gradually returned to her pupils and she recovered. Then, indeed, it was not so much that she got back the exterior vision of her eyes as that her inner rational insight was reformed, precisely through the twin novelty of this miracle.

The Life of Ida of Louvain, 1.38

Another of Ida's graces worth mentioning was that, after Communion, the gaze of her eyes would become so lightsome and bright that the objects on which she focused them would themselves begin to emit a brilliant glow, which you could observe for yourself, a glow comparable to, though of course less intense than, that of the sun. So brightly could that focal point shine that, on one occasion, when Ida had focused upon the chalice to drink from it, it shone out, and the priest mistook the shining for the falling of a ray of the sun upon it; but then he turned fully to Ida and directed his gaze to her face and so discovered that the glow had been coming from her eyes.

Nor was it only at Communion time that this happened to her; for there is evidence from some who have pursued the matter that it also happened on sundry other occasions. Thus Ida was once sitting with some others in the infirmary and pouring out spiritual words from the full storage vat of her heart, when a nun who was sitting opposite her looked attentively at her face and caught sight of certain fiery rays, like sunbeams, which the face was emitting and diffusing to all quarters. It was this nun's opinion, as far as her investigation had reached, that these rays had themselves been borrowed from the sun.

The Life of Ida of Louvain, 3.21

The following November, during the Octave of All Saints, Ida was in choir for Mass. Once again she and the space around her were lit up with an immense glow, as if all the beaming rays of the sun were concentrated there. The wall at which she was standing and on which she was lightly supporting herself, likewise had its surface brightly lit up by the glow reflected from herself. The rays had all the appearance of sunbeams, as if it were the sun that was shining on the wall. She thought someone might have come up behind her with something like a candle and been responsible for that light; so she glanced behind but saw no one. She moved to another viewpoint, only to find no difference at all in the lighting. She finally trained the whole focus of her eyes upon the crucifix, in memory of Christ's blessed Passion and of his embracing her, and in this way she was able to take joyful rest on the reclining couch of love.

The Life of Ida of Louvain, 3.23

Beatrice's frail body stood so firm in its own way that never in her whole life did she learn by experience what bad will or carnal affection or excitement or worldly delight was. Although her body was always and in everything obedient and subject to the spirit, in this one matter her body was an impediment: that her affection, impeded by this obstacle, could barely attain what it desired. Restrained by its mortality, her affection could not attain the everlasting fruition of the supreme Good which it sought. Her body, like a thin membrane which is easily broken or like a shining cloud which is easily penetrated by the clear radiance of the sun, seemed still to obstruct her spirit which was always aspiring upward. Once this cloud was dispelled there was nothing by which an obstacle of any sort could keep her spirit from being perpetually illuminated by the eternal sun. Therefore she implored in prayer that this thin membrane be speedily broken, and with fervent desire of the heart she persistently longed for the light little cloud to be driven away by the ray of the eternal sun.

The Life of Beatrice of Nazareth, 3.198

To you, Lord Jesus, how truly my heart has said: *My face looks to you. Lord, I do seek your face.*[1] In the dawn you brought me proof of your love, in my first approach to kiss your revered feet you forgave my evil ways as I lay in the dust. With the advancement of the day you gave your servant reason to rejoice when, in the kiss of the hand, you imparted the grace to live rightly. And now what remains, O good Jesus, except that suffused as I am with the fullness of your light, and while my spirit is fervent, you would graciously bestow on me the kiss of your mouth, and give me unbounded joy in your presence. Serenely lovable above all others, tell me where will you lead your flock to graze, where will you rest it at noon?[2]

Bernard of Clairvaux
Sermon 3 on the Song of Songs, 6

[1] *Ps 142:8*

[2] *Sg 1:6*

The vision that you ask for, Bride of mine, is above your capacity, you are as yet unable to gaze upon that sublime noontide brightness that is my dwelling place. You have asked where I pasture my flocks, the place where I rest at noon.[1] But to be drawn up through the clouds, to penetrate to where light is total, to plunge through seas of splendor and make your home where light is unapproachable,[2] that is beyond the scope of an earthly life or an earthly body. That is reserved for you at the end of all things, when I shall take you, all glorious, to myself, without spot or wrinkle or any such thing. Do you not know that as long as you live in the body you are exiled from the light?[3] With your beauty still incomplete how can you consider yourself fit to gaze on beauty in its totality? And why should you want to see me in my splendor, while you still do not know yourself? Because if you had a better knowledge of yourself you would know that, burdened with a perishable body, you cannot possibly lift up your eyes and fix them on this radiant light that the angels long to contemplate.[4] The time will come when I shall reveal myself, and your beauty will be complete, just as my beauty is complete; you will be so like me that you will see me as I am.

Bernard of Clairvaux
Sermon 38 on the Song of Songs, 5

[1] *Sg 1:6*   [3] *2 Cor 5:6*
[2] *1 Tm 6:16*   [4] *1 Pt 1:12*

The chalice of vision will be presented to you, the inebriating and very bright chalice[1] of the glory of the divine countenance; and you will drink from the torrent of divine voluptuousness, and you will become inebriated when the fountain of light itself refreshes you eternally in the delights of its fullness. Then you will see the heavens full of the indwelling glory of God and that virginal light giver that, after God, lights up the entire heaven with the brightness of its cleanest light, and the miraculous works of the fingers of God, and the morning stars that always so merrily stand before the face of God, ministering to him.[2]

Gertrud the Great of Helfta
Spiritual Exercises, 6

[1] *Lam 4:21*
[2] *Jb 38:7*

Let us return to ourselves, let us examine our paths; and in order to accomplish this in truth, let us invoke the Spirit of truth, let us call to him from the deep into which he has led us, because he leads us on the way by which we discover ourselves, and without him we can do nothing. Nor should we be afraid that he will disdain to come down to us, for the contrary is true: he is displeased if we attempt even the least thing without him. For he is not one who passes and does not return, he leads us on from brightness to brightness because he is the Spirit of the Lord.[1] Sometimes he fills us with rapture by communication of his light, sometimes he adapts himself to our weakness and sends beams of light into the dark about us.[2] But whether we are raised above ourselves or left with ourselves, let us stay always in the light, always walk as children of the light.[3]

Bernard of Clairvaux
Sermon 17 on the Song of Songs, 8

[1] *2 Cor 3:18*
[2] *Ps 17:29*
[3] *Eph 5:8*

Milk can go bad and the lily wither and snow become dirty, but no defilement can come into light. It will be inseparable from the man it glorifies, clinging to him like a robe of glory,[1] breathing forth innocence and containing within its own circumference the brightness of its holiness. For all eternity it will not see corruption, nor in the ages yet to come experience any diminution of its radiance. That garment of light is a garment indeed, a luminous garment, subject to no darkness, not afraid of spot or wrinkle, moth or wrinkle, burn or cut or anything similar. For it will know no trouble from the spot of another's evil or the wrinkle of its own duplicity, from the inborn moth of pride or the fretting old age of discontent, from the devouring burn of concupiscence or the cut of spite or discord.

The first to be clothed in this white robe is that young man, fairest among the sons of men,[2] who first of all triumphed over death and put on splendor, so that with reason the bride glories in him uniquely and says: 'My beloved is all radiant.'[3]

John of Forde
Sermon 3 on the Song of Songs, 5

[1] *Si 38:22*

[2] *Ps 45:2*

[3] *Sg 5:10*

When Aelred's body was laid naked before us to be washed, we saw how the glory to come had been revealed in him. His flesh was clearer than glass, whiter than snow, as though his members were those of a boy five years old, without a trace of stain, but altogether sweet, and composed and pleasant. There was no loss of hair to make him bald, his long illness had caused no distortion, fasting no pallor, tears had not bleared his eyes. Perfect in every part of his body, the dead father shone like a carbuncle, was fragrant as incense, pure and immaculate in the radiance of his flesh as a child. I was not able to restrain the kisses which I gave his feet, though I chose his feet lest affection rather than love should reproach me; the beauty of one who sleeps rather than delight in one who lies as he lay. Whenever I think of him then, I am still overcome by joy and wonder at the gracious recollection. And when do I not think of it? When do I not brood on that sweetness, that beauty, that glory? My God! he did not die in darkness, as those that have been long dead, not so, Lord, but in your light, for in his light we see your light.[1]

Walter Daniel
The Life of Aelred of Rievaulx, 58

[1] *Ps 35:10*

If anything of the heavenly light has shone on your eyes, be careful not to vaunt yourself on it as though you had escaped all the darkness of being blind. Do not let your speech make you into one of those who rebelled against the light by claiming: 'Surely we are not blind?' What you must do rather is to listen to the light, and submit humbly when he says to you: *For a little longer the light is with you. So while you have the light, believe in the light, that you may be sons of light.*[1] Blessed be God, who has given us a light to shine out of the darkness![2] But if we say that we have a great light in us, when really it is only a little light, we would have to fear that what was little would shrink from littleness to nothingness, and in a little while become darkness. If we would be worthy of being sons of light, then we must bewail the darkness which still closes us in on every side. If we are not to be blind, then we must feel no shame in admitting that, in fact, we are blind. There is great merit in God's eyes when a man sees his blindness, sees it, bitterly laments it, and takes it to Jesus to be healed.

John of Forde
Sermon 19 on the Song of Songs, 3

[1] *Jn 12:35-36*
[2] *2 Cor 4:6*

All of you are sons of light and sons of the day. We do not belong to the night or to the darkness.[1] For the night has passed away, the day has drawn near.[2] Although we were once darkness, now we are light in the Lord.[3] Nonetheless, if, because we are not darkness nor sons of the darkness, we say that we do not suffer anything of darkness, we are deceiving ourselves and bringing upon ourselves the darkness of death such as does not deserve to be enlightened. For what does the light of the world say, he who came into this world for judgment, in order that they who do not see may see, and they who see may become blind? 'Because you say: We see,' he says, 'your sin remains.' I see to some slight extent, because you enlighten my lamp, O Lord; but since what I see is not much, my God, enlighten my darkness.[4]

Guerric of Igny
Sermon 3 for the Epiphany, 2

[1] *1 Thes 5:5*

[2] *Rom 13:12*

[3] *Eph 5:8*

[4] *Ps 17:29*

These are the stages by which you should make progress, this is the way in which I think you should advance, O faithful soul, in order that you may cast off the darkness of this world and arrive at your home country of eternal brightness, where your darkness will be like midday[1] and night will be lit up like day.[2] Then indeed, then you will see and be radiant, your heart will thrill and rejoice, when the whole earth is filled with the majesty of unbounded light and his glory is seen in you.[3] House of Jacob, come and let us walk in the light of the Lord;[4] as sons of light let us walk[5] from brightness to brightness, with the Spirit of the Lord to go before us and by one degree of virtue after another let us enter further and further into the kingdom of brightness.

Guerric of Igny
Sermon 3 for the Epiphany, 4

[1] *Is 58:10*   [4] *Is 2:5*
[2] *Ps 138:12*   [5] *Eph 5:8*
[3] *Is 60:2*

There is something in a single word of what follows which, if we take it seriously, will move the intention of our heart either to right or to left. For what is more terrible to sinners or more desirable to the devout than to appear before the face of the Sun of justice shining with full strength. The prophet says of him, *Who will consider the day of his coming, or who will stand to see him.*[1]

His face, says John, was like the sun shining with full strength.[2] The psalmist who said, *Turn your face from my sins,*[3] was anxiously shrinking away from this face. Yet, filled with an equally great desire for that face he said, *My heart has said to you: My face has sought you; your face, O Lord, will I seek*[4]; and in another psalm he says, *When shall I come and appear before the face of the Lord?*[5]

Geoffrey of Auxerre
Sermon 7 on the Apocalypse

[1] *Mal 3:2*   [4] *Ps 27:8*

[2] *Rv 1:16*   [5] *Ps 42:1 [2]*

[3] *Ps 51:9*

His face is compared to the sun simply because nothing more splendid exists. For the sun shines with full strength[1] when no cloud of any sort blocks it, and it gleams in all the purity and fullness of its light. The moon shines too, but not in its own strength, because it does not shine of itself, they say, but by the sun's light. So also will the righteous shine like the sun in the kingdom of their Father.[2] They will shine in the Lord's strength, not their own, for as they see him as he is they become like him. How truly and fully blessed will the pure of heart be, because they will see God.

Meanwhile, I beg you, beloved, let us come into the presence of that face with thanksgiving, with the thanksgiving that cleanses the stains on our hearts that can block so blessed and beatific a vision.

Geoffrey of Auxerre
Sermon 7 on the Apocalypse

[1] *Rv 1:16*
[2] *Mt 13:43*

If we are willing to approach the darkness in which God himself is, having entered into the midst of the cloud,[1] stirred by the glory of such majesty, dismayed also by the immensity of that infinity, we shall not stand fast, we shall be as nothing. For *God dwells in light inaccessible;*[2] his fire devours the flesh like stubble; his face no man can see and live. The angels cannot fathom his depth; no power comes near to him except that which was united to the Word in the unity of Person. Therefore let us give glory to God and, falling on our faces, let us adore from afar the traces of the Trinity, believing in our hearts and confessing with our lips, for whatever we have thought or said concerning him is less than he is.

Amadeus of Lausanne
Homily 3 on the Praises of the Virgin Mary

[1] *Ex 24:18*
[2] *1 Tm 6:16*

The voice of Christ to the soul: 'Look upon me, my dove, at who I am: I am Jesus, your dulcet friend. Open to me the recesses of your heart. I am, indeed, from the land of angels, an exemplar of radiance.[1] I am myself the splendor of the divine sun.

'I am the most fulgent spring day, the only one that grows ever bright and knows no waning. The majesty of my super essential glory whose extent is measured only by eternity, fills heaven and earth. Only I wear on my head the imperial diadem of my glorious deity. I bear the garland of my rose-colored blood, which I spilled for you. Neither above nor below the sun is there anything like me.'[2]

Gertrud the Great of Helfta
Spiritual Exercises, 3

[1] *Ps 44:3*
[2] *Ex 15:11*

Even though the Sun increases in warmth and strength, though it multiplies and extends its rays over the whole course of our mortal lives, for it will be with us even to the end of the world, it will not attain to its noontide splendor, nor be seen here below in that fullness which it will exhibit hereafter, at least to those who are destined for the privilege of this vision. O true noontide, fullness of warmth and light, trysting-place of the sun; noontide that blots out shadows, that dries up marshes, that banishes evil odors! O perpetual solstice, day that will never decline to evening![1] O noontide light, with your springtime freshness, your summer-like gracefulness, your autumnal fruitfulness and—let me not seem to omit it—your winter of quiescence and leisure! Although, if you prefer it, winter alone of these is over and gone. Show me this place, she said, where there is so much brightness and peace and fullness.

So may I too merit the ecstatic grace of contemplating you in your light[2] and beauty, as you generously feed your flock and make them rest securely.

Bernard of Clairvaux
Sermon 33 on the Song of Songs, 6

[1] *Lk 24:29*
[2] *Is 33:17*

The Cistercian Authors

AELRED OF RIEVAULX

was born in 1110 in Hexham in Northumbria (Northern England). His father, like his grandfather, was a priest. After receiving a very good education, he became a page in the court of King David of Scotland. He was then appointed the bursar of the court. During a business trip, he discovered Rievaulx. He entered there at the age of twenty-four, and was successively director of novices, abbot of Revesby, a daughter-house of Rievaulx, and finally abbot of Rievaulx, a post he held for forty years. When he was novice director, Bernard of Clairvaux asked him to write a treatise on charity to show that the observances can foster, and not stifle, charity. The result was his *Mirror of Charity*, in which one can see his ability as a monastic educator. He wrote several other treatises and historical works before his death in 1167.

AMADEUS OF LAUSANNE

was born *c.* 1110 in Dauphiné, France. His father, the Lord of Hauterive, entered the cistercian abbey of Bonnevaux around 1119, taking his son Amadeus with him. After professing his vows, he left for Cluny, again accompanied by his son. Regretting this move, he returned to Bonnevaux and entrusted Amadeus to his brother, Conrad of Hohenstaufen, later to become the Holy Roman Emperor Conrad III. In 1125, however, Amadeus decided to enter the abbey of Clairvaux. After fourteen years there, Bernard sent him as abbot of Hautecombe. Appointed bishop of Lausanne in 1144, he died in 1159. The eight homilies on the Blessed Virgin Mary which survive were written while he was bishop.

BALDWIN OF FORDE

After completing his studies, Baldwin, a native of Devonshire (England), followed a clercial career, and served as an archdeacon before he entered the cistercian abbey of Forde in 1169. There he was elected abbot in 1175. He was appointed bishop of Worcester in 1180, and Archbishop of Canterbury four years later. He served as legate under Pope Lucius III. He died in 1190, in Syria, during the third crusade. His written works focused on the mystery of faith. Among his several treatises is one on the cenobitic life, in which he demonstrates how it is modeled on to the Trinitarian life.

BEATRICE OF NAZARETH

Born in 1200 in a well-to-do family, Beatrice was sent to the Beguines for her education and then entered the cistercian monastery of Bloemendaal, founded by her father. She was subsequently sent to the monastery of Rameya, where she had mystical experiences. In 1236, she moved on again, this time to the monastery of Nazareth, where she took care of the novices and was prioress for more than thirty years. Her treatise entitled *Seven Experiences of* Loving (*Minne*) was later translated from Flemish into Latin by an unknown scribe. She died in 1268.

BERNARD OF CLAIRVAUX

was born in 1090 at Fontaine, near Dijon in Burgundy, France, of noble parents. His five brothers trained for military careers, but Bernard's fragile health led his father to enroll him at the religious institute of Saint Vorles at Châtillon to receive instruction leading to an ecclesiastical career. After studying there for ten years and hesitating about his future, he finally decided to enter the abbey of Cîteaux in 1113, taking with him several of his relatives and friends. Two years later, he was sent to Clairvaux as the founding superior. Renowned as a reformer, he was often invited by councils of bishops to help carry out the policies of change within the Church. Civil authorities even consulted him in seeking solutions that would bring peace and justice. Of all his extensive writings, his Sermons on the Song of Songs are perhaps the best known and most beloved. He died in 1153.

GEOFFREY OF AUXERRE

As a student in Paris, Geoffrey heard Bernard of Clairvaux preach on conversion. This led him to leave Paris and enter Clairvaux, where he became Bernard's secretary and biographer. He himself became abbot of four successive monasteries. In addition to recording events in the life of Bernard, he composed a commentary on the book of Revelation.

GERTRUD OF HELFTA

In 1301, at the age of five, Gertrud was entrusted to the monastery of Helfta, in Germany, whose nuns followed the cistercian way of life. She loved studies and became erudite. She served her community as second chantress and as a copier of manuscripts. After having a vision of Christ when she was twenty-five, she focused her attention exclusively on union with Christ. Hoping to share the message confided to her, she wrote *Spiritual Exercises* and *The Herald of Divine Loving-kindness* (*pietas*). Liturgy is the foundation of her spirituality, which is based on a sound and carefully expressed theology. She died in her monastery in 1302.

GILBERT OF HOYLAND

This English monk was sent to the monastery of Swineshead, in Linconshire, where he was abbot for at least seventeen years. His *Sermons on the Song of Songs* took up the incomplete commentary begun by Bernard of Clairvaux. He died in 1172 in the monastery of Larivour, in France, probably on his way to the Cistercian General Chapter.

GREGORY THE GREAT

was born in Rome *c.* 550, in a wealthy family of senatorial rank. By 573, he was prefect of the city of Rome, the highest civil position of the time. A year later, however, he sold his patrimony, founded monasteries, transformed his family home into a monastery, and gave the rest of his wealth to the poor. In 579, Pope Pelagius sent him as *apocrisarius* (ambassador) to Constantinople. In 590 he was elected pope at a time of invasions and epidemics. In addition to many sermons on Scripture, he composed the famous *Dialogues*,containing all that is known of the life of Saint Benedict. He died in 604.

GUERRIC OF IGNY

studied in the cathedral school of Tournai (Belgium), the city where he was born *c.* 1087. After leading this same school for a while, he chose a life of solitude and prayer in an adjacent house. Hearing about Bernard, he visited Clairvaux and decided to join. After thirteen years, Bernard sent him as abbot to Igny, in Champagne, in 1138. There he died in 1157. Fifty-four of his sermons of the liturgical year have survived.

ISAAC OF STELLA

Born in England *c.* 1110, Isaac went to study in France with Peter Abelard and Gilbert of Poitiers. Although he was a brilliant philosopher and theologian, he renounced an ecclesiastical career to become a cistercian monk, perhaps at Pontigny. Abbot of the monastery of Stella (L'Etoile), near Poitiers, in 1147, he spent some time on the island of Ré. Into his sermons he introduces metaphysical elements learned at the schools.

JOHN OF FORDE

Born in Devonshire c. 1140, John entered the monastery of Forde, and served as Baldwin's secretary. He became in turn prior of Forde, abbot of Bindon, and finally, in 1192, abbot of Forde during a difficult time in the relationship between the crown and the Churchs. His one hundred twenty Sermons on the Song of Songs continue and, in a very personal style, complete the commentary begun and continued by Bernard and Gilbert. He died in 1214.

WILLIAM OF SAINT THIERRY

Born in Liége of a noble family in the second half of the eleventh century, William may have studied at Laon under Master Anselm before entering the benedictine monastery of Saint Nicaise in Rheims. Around 1220, he became abbot of Saint Thierry outside the city. At roughly the same time he met Bernard of Clairvaux and a deep friendship formed between them. Although he asked to enter Clairvaux, Bernard firmly encouraged him to remain in charge of his brothers. Nevertheless, they communicated often and helped one another in their literary and spiritual works. Among William's many treatises, is a small work on *The Contemplation of God*. After serving as abbot for fourteen years, he finally retired to the newly founded cistercian abbey of Signy. He later visited the carthusian charter house of Mont Dieu and to these brothers he addressed his famous *Golden Epistle*. He died in 1148, leaving unfinished the Life of Saint Bernard he had begun.

Further Reading
in the Fathers

Published in the Cistercian Fathers Series by Cistercian Publications
unless otherwise noted.

Aelred of Rievaulx: Liturgical Sermons. The First Clairvaux Collection.
Translated by Theodore Berkeley and M. Basil Pennington. Cistercian Fathers 58. Kalamazoo, 2001.

Aelred of Rievaulx: The Mirror of Charity. Translated by Elizabeth Connor. Cistercian Fathers 17. Kalamazoo, 1990.

Amadeus of Lausanne. Homilies in Praise of Blessed Mary. Translated by Grace Perrigo. Cistercian Fathers 18B. Kalamazoo, 1998.

Baldwin of Forde. Spiritual Tractates. Two volumes. Translated by David N. Bell. Cistercian Fathers 38, 41. Kalamazoo, 1986.

Bernard of Clairvaux: Homilies in Praise of the Blessed Virgin Mary.
Translated by Marie-Bernard Saïd. Cistercian Fathers 18A. Kalamazoo: Cistercian Publications, 1993. Originally published as *Bernard of Clairvaux: Treatises 3.* Kalamazoo, 1977.

The Letters of Saint Bernard of Clairvaux. Translated by Bruno Scott James. London, 1953. Revised edition, Cistercian Studies 62. Kalamazoo, 1998.

Bernard of Clairvaux: Sermons on the Song of Songs. Translated by Killian Walsh and Irene Edmonds. 4 volumes. Cistercian Fathers 4, 7, 31, 40. Spencer–Kalamazoo, 1971, 1976, 1979, 1980.

Bernard of Clairvaux. Sermons for Advent and the Christmas Season. Translated by Irene Edmonds, Wendy Beckett, Conrad Greenia. Cistercian Fathers 51. Kalamazoo, 2007.

Geoffrey of Auxerre. On the Apocalypse. Translated by Joseph Gibbons. Cistercian Fathers 42. Kalamazoo, 2000.

Gertrud the Great of Helfta: The Herald of God's Loving-Kindness. Translated by Alexandra Barratt. Cistercian Fathers 35 and 63. Kalamazoo, 1991, 1999.

Gertrud the Great of Helfta: Spiritual Exercises. Translated by Gertrud Jaron Lewis and Jack Lewis. Cistercian Fathers 49. Kalamazoo, 1989.

Gilbert of Hoyland. Sermons on the Song of Songs. Three volumes. Translated by Lawrence C. Braceland. Cistercian Fathers 14, 20, 26. Kalamazoo, 1978, 1979.

Gregory the Great, *The Life of Saint Benedict*, Book Two of the *Dialogues.* Translated by Leonard Doyle. Collegeville: Liturgical Press, 1948.

Guerric of Igny: Liturgical Sermons. Two volumes. Translated by Monks of Mount Saint Bernard Abbey. Cistercian Fathers, 8, 32. Spencer, 1970, 1971.

Isaac of Stella. Sermons on the Christian Year, volume 1 [of 2]. Translated by Hugh McCaffery. Cistercian Fathers Kalamazoo: Cistercian Publications, 1979. Volume 2 (CF 66) is projected.

The Life of Beatrice of Nazareth. Translated by Roger De Ganck. Cistercian Fathers 50. Kalamazoo, 1991.

The Life of Ida of Louvain. Translated by Martinus Cawley. Guadalupe, Oregon: Guadalupe Translations, 1990.

John of Ford[e]. *Sermons on the Final Verses of The Song of Songs*. Seven volumes. Translated by Wendy Mary Beckett. CF 29, 39, 43-47. Kalamazoo, 1977, 1982, 1983, 1984.

Walter Daniel. The Life of Aelred of Rievaulx. Translated by F. M. Powicke. London, 1950. Revised edition. Cistercian Fathers 57. Kalamazoo, 1994.

William of Saint Thierry: On Contemplating God, Prayer, Meditations. Translated by Penelope Lawson. Cistercian Fathers 3. Spencers, 1970.

Index

123